KEYNOTE guide to
topics in your course

CLIFFS KEYNOTE REVIEWS

French Grammar

by

ANNE HELGESEN

Cedar Crest College

CLIFF'S NOTES, INC. • LINCOLN, NEBRASKA 68501

ISBN   0-8220-1724-5

L.C. Catalogue Card Number: 77–89835

Printed in the United States of America

CONTENTS

TO THE STUDENT

This KEYNOTE is a flexible study aid designed to help you REVIEW YOUR COURSE QUICKLY and USE YOUR TIME TO STUDY ONLY MATERIAL YOU DON'T KNOW.

FOR GENERAL REVIEW

Take the SELF-TEST on the first page of any topic and turn the page to check your answers.

Read the EXPLANATIONS of any questions you answered incorrectly.

If you are satisfied with your understanding of the material, move on to another topic.

If you feel that you need further review, read the column of BASIC FACTS. For a more detailed discussion of the material, read the column of ADDITIONAL INFORMATION.

FOR QUICK REVIEW

Read the column of BASIC FACTS for a rapid review of the essentials of a topic and then take the SELF-TEST if you want to test your understanding of the material.

ADDITIONAL HELP FOR EXAMS

Test yourself by taking the sample FINAL EXAM.

1 ARTICLES, NOUNS, PARTITIVE, POSSESSION

DIRECTIONS: Select the appropriate form of the article or noun for each of the following sentences, and write your answers (a, b, or c) on the numbered lines to the right. To check your answers, turn to page 3. Study the explanations for any questions you missed.

1. *Il descendait vers _____ ponts.*
   a *le*
   b *la*
   c *les*

2. *Il a donné son livre _____ garçon.*
   a *à la*
   b *au*
   c *à l'*

3. *Il avait _____ très long trajet à faire.*
   a *un*
   b *une*
   c *des*

4. *Il y a _____ choses intéressantes à voir.*
   a *du*
   b *de la*
   c *des*

5. *C'est un bon _____.*
   a *professeur*
   b *exemples*
   c *mère*

6. *Voilà une grande _____.*
   a *arbre*
   b *chien*
   c *maison*

7. *Il y a des _____ dans la rue.*
   a *homme*
   b *étudiant*
   c *voitures*

8. *Avez-vous _____ argent?*
   a *du*
   b *de l'*
   c *des*

9. *Elle n'a pas _____ amis.*
   a *d'*
   b *des*
   c *de*

10. *J'ai _____ bon tabac.*
    a *de la*
    b *de*
    c *du*

11. *Il a _____ gros ennuis.*
    a *des*
    b *de*
    c *de la*

12. *Nous avons beaucoup _____ temps.*
    a *de*
    b *du*
    c *des*

1 _____
2 _____
3 _____
4 _____
5 _____
6 _____
7 _____
8 _____
9 _____
10 _____
11 _____
12 _____

BASIC FACTS

THE DEFINITE ARTICLE

	MASC.	FEM.
SING.	le, l'	la, l'
PLUR.	les	les

le mari	*la femme*
les maris	*les femmes*

L' is used before a singular noun beginning with a vowel or a silent *h,* whether masculine or feminine.

l'homme	*l'île*
l'arbre	*l'héroïne*

Although *h* is never pronounced in French, it is sometimes counted as a consonant; in that case it takes the usual singular article.

le héros	*la hache*

This is called an aspirate *h* and occurs mainly in words of Germanic origin.

CONTRACTIONS

	MASC.	FEM.
SING.	au, à l'	à la, à l'
PLUR.	aux	aux

The preposition *à* (to, at) combines with the definite article in the masculine singular and with plural articles.

au garçon	*à la soeur*
aux garçons	*aux soeurs*

The form *à l'* is required before a singular noun beginning with a vowel or a silent *h.*

à l'homme	*à l'île*

In the same way *de* (of, from) combines with the definite masculine singular article and with plural articles.

du garçon	*de la soeur*
des garçons	*des soeurs*

The form *de l'* is used before a singular noun beginning with a vowel or a silent *h.*

(Continued on page 4)

ADDITIONAL INFORMATION

THE DEFINITE ARTICLE

The definite article is used in the singular to indicate a specific noun, as in English. It is also necessary for countries, languages, etc.: *la France, le Canada, le français.* It is normally required even when the meaning is general.

Les hommes de cette famille sont intelligents. (specific)
Les hommes sont plus intelligents que les animaux. (general)
L'homme est un être humain. (general)

Following the subject, the definite article should be used for parts of the body and clothing.

Il met la main dans la poche.   Elle se lave les pieds.

It is required for titles, qualified proper nouns, and dates.

le professeur	*le petit Charles*	*le 30 novembre*
	Smith	

It is used for days of the week only when it means "every."

Les musées se ferment le lundi.

OMISSION OF THE ARTICLE

There should be no article before a title used in direct speech, most names of towns, nouns in enumerations, two nouns used adjectivally, or an unqualified or well-known noun in apposition.

Bonjour, Professeur!
Il vient de Paris et il va à New York.
Nous avons vu hommes, femmes, et enfants, tous morts.
C'est une table de bois.
Louis XIV, roi de France, mourut en 1715.

The article is also omitted when presenting an unmodified term of occupation, rank, nationality, or religion.

Il est étudiant.	*Il est devenu maire.*
Il est français.	*Elle est catholique.*

THE PARTITIVE

The preposition *de* plus the definite article is used in the partitive sense in the singular and plural.

J'ai acheté du pain.   Voulez-vous des bonbons?

De appears alone before a plural adjective preceding a noun (unless the adjective forms part of the noun as in *jeune fille, des jeunes filles*), after a negative expression if the meaning is "not any," or after most expressions of quantity.

Il voit de belles choses.   Je n'ai pas d'argent.
Elle a tant de choses à faire.

The two exceptions among the expressions of quantity are *la plupart* and *bien.*

(Continued on page 4)

EXPLANATIONS

1. *Il descendait vers **les** ponts*. A plural noun requires a plural article.

2. *Il a donné son livre **au** garçon*. The noun *garçon* is masculine singular. The preposition *à* combines with the masculine singular article *le* to form *au*.

3. *Il avait **un** très long trajet à faire*. The noun *trajet* is masculine and singular; therefore, it requires the masculine singular article.

4. *Il y a **des** choses intéressantes à voir*. Because the noun *choses* is plural, it takes the plural indefinite article, which is a combination of *de* plus *les*.

5. *C'est un bon **professeur**.* The article and adjective are both masculine singular, thus requiring a masculine singular noun.

6. *Voilà une grande **maison**.* The feminine singular article and adjective need a feminine singular noun.

7. *Il y a des **voitures** dans la rue*. The plural indefinite article takes a plural noun.

8. *Avez-vous **de** l'argent?* The singular noun begins with a vowel and thus requires the *l'* form of the article.

9. *Elle n'a pas **d'**amis*. After a negative and when the meaning is "not any," the partitive article is reduced to *de* (or *d'* before a noun that begins with a vowel).

10. *J'ai **du** bon tabac*. Because the noun *tabac* is masculine and singular, it needs the masculine singular article.

11. *Il a **de** gros ennuis*. When a plural adjective precedes a plural noun, *de* is normally used alone.

12. *Nous avons beaucoup **de** temps*. After an expression of quantity *de* is normally used without the definite article.

Answers

c	1
b	2
a	3
c	4
a	5
c	6
c	7
b	8
a	9
c	10
b	11
a	12

de l'homme   de l'île

These forms of *de* also appear in the partitive sense meaning "some."

THE INDEFINITE ARTCLE

	MASC.	FEM.
SING.	un	une
PLUR.	des	des

un tapis   une maison
des tapis   des maisons

NOUNS

All nouns in French are either masculine or feminine: *le père, la mère.* Names of objects usually retain the gender of the word from which they originated; this gender should be memorized along with the word.

MASC.	FEM.
le lit	*la table*
un lit	*une table*

Most feminine nouns end in *-e*, but there are a number of exceptions: *le livre, le pupitre, l'homme, le frère,* etc.

To form the plural of a noun, *-s* is generally added, but some nouns add an *-x*.

	MASC.	FEM.
SING.	le garçon	la mère
	un garçon	une mère
PLUR.	les garçons	les mères
	des garçons	des mères
But:	le bureau	la peau
	un bureau	une peau
	les bureaux	les peaux
	des bureaux	des peaux

POSSESSION

The preposition *de* indicates possession and contracts with the definite article mentioned previously.

Voilà le lit de Paul.
Voyez-vous l'auto du professeur?
Voici les gants de la mère.
Voici les livres du frère de la jeune fille.

La plupart du temps...   La plupart des gens...
Après bien de la peine...   Bien des fois...

The article is normally omitted after *avec* and *sans.*

Il l'a fait avec difficulté.   Il est revenu sans argent.

THE INDEFINITE ARTICLE

The plural indefinite article is more common than in English, which often omits the word "some."

Il y a des oeufs sur la table.

GENDER OF NOUNS

If a noun indicates a person, the sex usually determines the gender.

un homme, une femme   un étudiant, une étudiante

However, some French nouns do not have a feminine form.

un enfant, une enfant   un collègue, une collègue

Some nouns are always masculine: *un professeur.* Some nouns are always feminine: *la connaissance, la dupe, la personne, la recrue, la vedette, la victime.*

FEMININE NOUNS

Most nouns ending in *-e, -é,* and *-on* are feminine.

la rose, l'université, la flatterie, la saison, la nation

However, there are exceptions, and these should be memorized as they occur.

MASCULINE NOUNS

Most masculine nouns end in a consonant.

le lit, le tapis, l'amour, le travail

Some groups of words ending in *-acle, -age, -amme, -eau, -ège, -ème, -ète, -ice,* and *-isme* are usually masculine.

le miracle, le sage, le programme, le pinceau, le privilège, le thème, le poète, le vice, le patriotisme

But of course there are exceptions.

PLURALS OF NOUNS

Most nouns add an *-s* to form the plural: *les étudiants, les étudiantes.* Nouns that already have an *-s* in the singular remain the same in the plural: *le bras, les bras.* Nouns ending in *-au* or *-eu* usually add an *-x* to form the plural.

le château, les châteaux   le feu, les feux

Nouns ending in *-al* or *-ail* change to *-aux* in the plural.

le cheval, les chevaux   le travail, les travaux

POSSESSION

Possession may also be indicated by using the verb *être,* the possessive adjective, or the possessive pronoun.

Ce livre est à Robert.   Ces films sont à moi.
Voilà son livre.   Voilà mes films.
Voici le sien.   Voici les miens.

PRESENT INDICATIVE TENSE, NUMBERS

DIRECTIONS: Complete each of the following examples by writing the correct present indicative form of the verb on the numbered lines to the right.

1. *Nous* _____. (*donner*—to give)

2. *Ils* _____. (*finir*—to finish)

3. *Vous* _____. (*venir*—to come)

4. *Je* _____. (*vendre*—to sell)

5. *Elle* _____. (*rompre*—to break)

6. *Tu* _____. (*avoir*—to have)

7. *Elles* _____. (*recevoir*—to receive)

8. *Il* _____. (*être*—to be)

Select the correct cardinal or ordinal numeral, and write your answers (a, b, or c) on the numbered lines to the right.

9. *Aujourd'hui c'est le* _____ (third) *juin.*
   a *trois*   b *troisième*
      c *treizième*

10. *Louis* _____ (Fourteenth) *mourut en 1715.*
    a *Quarante*   b *Quatorzième*
         c *Quatorze*

11. *Il y avait beaucoup de problèmes au* _____ (twelfth) *siècle.*
    a *deuxième*   b *douzième*
         c *douze*

12. *Vous avez mangé deux* _____ (thirds) *du gâteau.*
    a *trois*   b *tiers*   c *troisièmes*

13. *Je vois au moins trois* _____ (hundred) *personnes.*
    a *cents*   b *cent*   c *centaines*

14. *Il a* _____ (sixty-one) *ans.*
    a *soixante-un*   b *soixante-et-unième*
         c *soixante-et-un*

15. *C'est la* _____ (eighty-seventh) *fois.*
    a *quatre-vingt-sept*
       b *quatre-vingt-septième*
          c *quatre-vingt-septièmes*

1 _____

2 _____

3 _____

4 _____

5 _____

6 _____

7 _____

8 _____

9 _____

10 _____

11 _____

12 _____

13 _____

14 _____

15 _____

BASIC FACTS

1ST CONJUGATION: *-er* VERBS

donner (to give)

je	donn**e**	(I give, do give, am giving)
tu	donn**es**	(you give, etc.)
il (elle)	donn**e**	(he, she gives, etc.)
nous	donn**ons**	(we give, etc.)
vous	donn**ez**	(you give, etc.)
ils (elles)	donn**ent**	(they give, etc.)

The boldface endings may be added to the stem of any *-er* verb. This is by far the largest group of French verbs; any new verbs added to the language belong to this conjugation.

2ND CONJUGATION: *-ir* VERBS

First group: Second group:
  finir (to finish)   *venir* (to come)

je	fin**is**	je	viens
tu	fin**is**	tu	viens
il (elle)	fin**it**	il (elle)	vient
nous	fin**issons**	nous	ven**ons**
vous	fin**issez**	vous	ven**ez**
ils (elles)	fin**issent**	ils (elles)	vienn**ent**

Most *-ir* verbs belong to the first group, but it is important to learn which group each *-ir* verb belongs to.

3RD CONJUGATION: *-re* VERBS

vendre (to sell)

je	vend**s**
tu	vend**s**
il (elle)	vend (some verbs have **t**)
nous	vend**ons**
vous	vend**ez**
ils (elles)	vend**ent**

4TH CONJUGATION: *-oir* VERBS

devoir   *recevoir*
  (must, to owe)   (to receive)

je	dois	je	reçois
tu	dois	tu	reçois
il (elle)	doit	il (elle)	reçoit
nous	dev**ons**	nous	recev**ons**
vous	dev**ez**	vous	recev**ez**
ils (elles)	doiv**ent**	ils (elles)	reçoiv**ent**

(*Continued on page 8*)

ADDITIONAL INFORMATION

The present indicative tense serves much the same purpose in French as in English—it states or indicates a fact at the present time. Other words, however, are not added to the main verb in French to give the various meanings of the present tense.

THE INTERROGATIVE FORM

A question may be asked in two ways in French. One is by starting with the phrase *Est-ce que...* "Is it (true, a fact) that . . ."

> *Est-ce qu'il donne de l'argent à sa mère?*
> *Est-ce que Jean et Marie viennent aujourd'hui?*
> *Est-ce que vous avez le temps de le faire?*
> *Est-ce que nous sommes à l'heure?*

The second way is by reversing the verb and its pronoun subject, and connecting them with a hyphen.

> *Vient-il maintenant?*
> *Vont-elles en ville?*
> *Lui donne-**t**-il les livres?*

NOTE 1: For the 3rd person singular of *-er* verbs, a *t* must be inserted between the two vowels to make a smoother sound.

NOTE 2: For the 1st person singular of *-er* verbs, the form *est-ce que* is preferred.

> *Est-ce que je rentre avec lui?*

THE NEGATIVE FORM

All French negatives have two parts, but this does not mean that they are double negatives. Instead of saying "no one" the French say "not anyone"; instead of "nothing" they say "not anything," etc. "Not" is *ne... pas*. To make a sentence negative in French, place the first part of the negative (which is always *ne*) after the subject (pronoun or noun) and the second part of the negative after the verb. If the verb begins with a vowel, *ne* becomes *n'*.

> *Il **ne** donne **pas** son livre à Pierre.*
> *Jean **n'**arrive **pas** aujourd'hui*

THE NEGATIVE-INTERROGATIVE FORM

Simply combine the two forms, first by reversing the verb and pronoun, and then by placing the negative before and after the verb (plus pronoun).

> *Ne vient-il **pas** aujourd'hui?*
> *N'arrive-t-elle **pas** bientôt?*

(*Continued on page 8*)

EXPLANATIONS

1. *Nous **donnons.*** The regular ending of almost all French verbs in the 1st person plural is *-ons.*

2. *Ils **finissent.*** Many verbs whose infinitives end in *-ir* add *iss* to the stem in the plural. The regular ending of the 3rd person plural, *-ent,* is then added in this case.

3. *Vous **venez.*** A number of verbs whose infinitives end in *-ir* do not add *iss* in the plural. The regular ending for the 2nd person plural is *-ez.*

4. *Je **vends.*** The regular 1st person singular ending for all verbs of the 2nd, 3rd, and 4th conjugations is *-s.* For the 1st conjugation (*-er* verbs) it is *-e.*

5. *Elle **rompt.*** When a verb whose infinitive ends in *-re* has no *d* or *t* in the stem, it adds one to the 3rd person singular.

6. *Tu **as.*** The ending for the 2nd person singular of all French verbs is *-s.*

7. *Elles **reçoivent.*** Verbs whose infinitives end in *-oir* are very irregular and should be studied carefully.

8. *Il **est.*** The auxiliary verbs *avoir* and *être* are quite irregular and should be learned thoroughly.

9. *Aujourd'hui c'est le **trois** juin.* Cardinal numbers are used for dates in French.

10. *Louis **Quatorze** mourut en 1715.* Cardinal numbers are required for titles in French. Since it is part of a title, the number is capitalized.

11. *Il y avait beaucoup de problèmes au **douzième** siècle.* This is a straightforward use of the ordinal numeral, as in English.

12. *Vous avez mangé deux **tiers** du gâteau.* There are irregular forms for half, third, and fourth (or quarter) in French.

13. *Je vois au moins trois **cents** personnes.* When *cent* is plural and is not followed by another number, it adds an *-s.*

14. *Il a **soixante-et-un** ans.* For 21, 31, 41, 51, and 61, French adds *et.*

15. *C'est la **quatre-vingt-septième** fois.* The simple ordinal form of the numeral is called for here, as in English.

Answers

donnons	1
finissent	2
venez	3
vends	4
rompt	5
as	6
reçoivent	7
est	8
a	9
c	10
b	11
b	12
a	13
c	14
b	15

Few verbs are alike in this conjugation, but since this group is small it is best to learn each verb separately. If the vowel changes to an *a, o,* or *u,* a preceding *c* must add a cedilla to keep its soft sound. Notice that the verbs of all four conjugations have the same plural endings.

AUXILIARY VERBS

avoir (to have)		*être* (to be)	
j'	ai	je	suis
tu	as	tu	es
il (elle)	a	il (elle)	est
nous	av**ons**	nous	sommes
vous	av**ez**	vous	êtes
ills (elles)	ont	ils (elles)	sont

Observe particularly the forms of the 3rd personal plural.

CARDINAL NUMERALS

un (une), deux, trois, quatre, cinq, six, sept, huit, neuf, dix, onze, douze, treize, quatorze, quinze, seize, dix-sept, dix-huit, dix-neuf

vingt, vingt-et-un, vingt-deux, etc.
trente, trente-et-un, trente-deux, etc.
quarante, quarante-et-un, etc.
cinquante, cinquante-et-un, etc.
soixante, soixante-et-un, etc.
soixante-dix, soixante-onze, etc.
quatre-vingts, quatre-vingt-un, etc.
quatre-vingt-dix, quatre-vingt-onze, etc.
cent, cent un, cent deux, etc.
deux cents, deux cent un, etc.
mille (1000), deux mille, etc.
un million, deux millions, etc.

ORDINAL NUMERALS

premier (première), deuxième, troisième, quatrième, etc.

NOTE: *moitié* (half), *tiers* (third), and *quart* (quarter or fourth) are used for sizes and shares. *Moitié* is feminine; the others are masculine. *Second(e) is* used for the second of two, while *deuxième* refers to the second of a series.

If the subject is a noun, place the noun first and then construct the sentence in the usual way, or use *Est-ce que* before the simple sentence.

*Jean, **ne** rentre-t-il **pas** de bonne heure?*
*Est-ce que Marie **ne** l'aime **pas?***

NUMERICAL EXPRESSIONS

Notice how French numbers are used in the following examples:

les quatre premiers mois
les six dernières semaines
en premier lieu

Distance

Combien (Quelle distance) y a-t-il de Paris à Nice?
Notre ville se trouve à 200 kilomètres de Paris.

Size

Le salon a 6 mètres de long.
Le salon est long de 6 mètres.
Le salon a 6 mètres de long sur 4 de large.

Dates, Titles

Only cardinal numbers are used for dates and titles, except *premier (-ère)*.

Samedi sera le quatre juin.
Louis Quatorze était un roi célèbre.
Mon anniversaire est mardi le premier mai.
François Premier est un autre roi célèbre.

COLLECTIVES

une douzaine (de)	a dozen
une vingtaine (de)	a score (20)
une trentaine (de)	about 30
une quarantaine (de)	about 40
une centaine (de)	about 100
des centaines (de)	hundreds (of)
un millier (de)	about 1000
des milliers (de)	thousands (of)
un million (de)	a million
des millions (de)	millions (of)

MONTHS

janvier	January
février	February
mars	March
avril	April
mai	May
juin	June
juillet	July
août	August
septembre	September
octobre	October
novembre	November
décembre	December

DAYS OF THE WEEK

lundi (Monday), *mardi* (Tuesday), *mercredi* (Wednesday), *jeudi* (Thursday), *vendredi* (Friday), *samedi* (Saturday), *dimanche* (Sunday)

All days and months are masculine in French and are written with a small initial letter.

3   ADJECTIVES, POSSESSIVE ADJECTIVES

DIRECTIONS: Match each of the following nouns with an adjective selected from the list below, and write your answers on the numbered lines to the right.

1. *une _____ fleur*   *intéressant*

2. *des frères _____*   *curieuse*

3. *un homme _____*   *jolie*

4. *deux femmes _____*   *frais*

5. *un _____ garçon*   *grandes*

6. *les _____ maisons*   *terrible*

7. *une chose _____*   *meilleur*

8. *le _____ choix*   *intelligents*

9. *un orage _____*   *grand*

10. *du pain _____*   *heureuses*

For each of the following sentences, write T (True) on the line to the right if the possessive adjective is correct and write F (False) if it is incorrect.

11. *Son frère est intéressant.*

12. *Leurs mères sont vieilles.*

13. *Ma livre est difficile.*

14. *Ton auto est belle.*

15. *Notre maisons se trouvent très loin.*

16. *Vos nez vous fait mal?*

17. *Leur soeur a dix ans.*

18. *Son mère est gentille.*

19. *Votre ami vous aime.*

20. *Mes soeurs sont grandes.*

1	
2	
3	
4	
5	
6	
7	
8	
9	
10	
11	
12	
13	
14	
15	
16	
17	
18	
19	
20	

BASIC FACTS

Adjectives

	MASC.	FEM.
SING.	grand	grande
PLUR.	grands	grandes
SING.	vrai	vraie
PLUR.	vrais	vraies

Most adjectives, like nouns, add *-e* for the feminine and *-s* for the plural. Adjectives ending in an *-e* in the masculine remain the same in the feminine.

jeune	*jeune*
jeunes	*jeunes*

Adjectives that end in *-x* usually have a feminine form ending in *-se*. An *-x* in the masculine singular does not change in the plural.

heureux	*heureuse*
heureux	*heureuses*

Some adjectives ending in *-x* have an irregular feminine form.

roux	*rousse*
roux	*rousses*

Adjectives agree in number and gender with the noun or nouns they modify.

un grand ami	*une grande maison*
les grands garçons	*les petites filles*

If the nouns are not of the same gender, the plural adjective takes the masculine form. The masculine noun usually comes first.

Mon père et ma mère sont grands.
Les enfants sont indépendants.

Position of Adjectives

Unlike English usage, most French adjectives follow the noun. However, a number of short, common adjectives such as *petit, grand, jeune, vieux, joli, beau, bon, mauvais,* and *nouveau* are habitually placed before the noun.

(Continued on page 12)

ADDITIONAL INFORMATION

Unusual Forms

Some feminine forms of adjectives are unlike others, although they, too, end in *-e*.

MASC.	FEM.	MASC.	FEM.
aigu	*aiguë*	*grec*	*grecque*
favori	*favorite*	*public*	*publique*
malin	*maligne*	*roux*	*rousse*

Demi and *nu* vary as adjectives, but not in compound expressions when they precede the noun.

une demi-heure	*deux heures et demie*
nu-pieds	*les jambes nues*

Adjectives Used as Nouns

Frequently, adjectives appear alone, and the sense of the noun is given by the number and gender.

les pauvres	*les riches*	*les vieux*
les Françaises	*les émigrés*	*les petites*

Position of Adjectives

Some adjectives may precede *or* follow the noun. Usually when they precede, the meaning is figurative. If the adjectives follow, the meaning is literal.

un ancien ami (former)	*un château ancien* (ancient)
un certain homme (certain)	*un succès certain* (sure)
un cher ami (dear)	*une robe chère* (expensive)
un grand général (great)	*un général grand* (tall)
le même jour (same)	*la maison même* (itself)
un mauvais temps (unpleasant)	*un homme mauvais* (evil)
ma propre chambre (own)	*une chambre propre* (clean)
un simple animal (mere)	*une robe simple* (simple)

Even adjectives that normally follow nouns may be placed before them if closely connected in meaning.

la magnifique cathédrale de Notre-Dame
le célèbre President Wilson
une terrible affaire

They may also precede the noun if the meaning is figurative or complimentary.

de noires pensées
d'amers souvenirs
sa charmante femme
votre dévoué ami

(Continued on page 12)

EXPLANATIONS

1. *une **jolie** fleur*
Flower is feminine singular, and the adjective *jolie* precedes the noun.

2. *des frères **intelligents***
The noun is masculine plural, and *intelligents,* like most French adjectives, follows the noun and agrees with it in number and gender.

3. *un homme **intéressant***
The adjective is masculine singular and follows the noun.

4. *deux femmes **heureuses***
The feminine plural adjective follows and agrees with the noun.

5. *un **grand** garçon*
The adjective *grand* precedes the noun and is masculine singular.

6. *les **grandes** maisons*
The adjective is feminine plural in order to agree with the noun.

7. *une chose **curieuse***
This feminine singular adjective follows the noun.

8. *le **meilleur** choix*
This adjective precedes the noun and agrees with it.

9. *un orage **terrible***
The masculine singular adjective follows the noun.

10. *du pain **frais***
The masculine singular adjective follows the noun.

11. *Son,* being masculine singular, is correct for the noun *frère.*

12. *Leurs* is plural and agrees with *mères.* It has no distinct feminine form.

13. *Ma* is incorrect since *livre* as used here is masculine. *Mon* would be the correct form.

14. *Ton* is correct, for, although *auto* is feminine singular, it begins with a vowel and therefore needs the masculine form to make the liaison *ton‿auto.*

15. *Notre* is incorrect because *maisons* is plural. *Nos* should be used.

16. *Vos* is incorrect because *nez* here is singular. *Votre* would be correct.

17. *Leur* is correct with *soeur* because it has no separate feminine form.

18. *Son mère* is incorrect because "mother" remains feminine even if she is "his" mother. *Sa* is required.

19. *Votre* is correct with the singular *ami,* whether masculine or feminine *(amie).*

20. *Mes soeurs* is correct. Both adjective and noun are plural.

Answers	
jolie	1
intelligents	2
intéressant	3
heureuses	4
grand	5
grandes	6
curieuse	7
meilleur	8
terrible	9
frais	10
T	11
T	12
F	13
T	14
F	15
F	16
T	17
F	18
T	19
T	20

une grande maison une jolie femme
un bon repas   une mauvaise nuit

Two adjectives qualifying a noun usually keep their normal position.

une grande maison blanche
un bon repas français

Two adjectives following a noun are linked by *et*.

un discours difficile et ennuyeux
une voix monotone et désagréable

Some adjectives have three forms in the singular.

	MASC.	FEM.
SING.	beau, bel	belle
PLUR.	beaux	belles

Similarly *nouveau, vieux,* and *fou* have an extra masculine form: *nouvel, vieil,* and *fol.* These additional forms are used only for a masculine noun beginning with a vowel or a mute *h*.

un bel esprit   *un nouvel état*
un vieil homme   *un fol espoir*

POSSESSIVE ADJECTIVES

MASC.	FEM.	PLURAL
mon	ma	mes
ton	ta	tes
son	sa	ses
notre	notre	nos
votre	votre	vos
leur	leur	leurs

Possessive adjectives replace articles and, like them, must be used for each noun mentioned.

mon père et ma mère
votre oncle et votre tante

The masculine singular form is required before a noun, whether masculine or feminine, that begins with a vowel or a mute *h*.

mon idée son expérience ton hôtel

But before an aspirate *h* beginning a feminine word, the feminine adjective is necessary.

ma hache   sa honte   ta haie

Tout and *quel* habitually precede the noun. *Tout* also precedes the article.

toute la famille   tout le monde

Without the article, *tout* means "any" or "every."

Toute femme aime les bijoux.
Tout homme est aventureux.

Quel normally appears without an article.

Quel homme!   *Quels enfants!*
Quelle maison est-ce? *A quel jour sommes-nous?*

Tout, when used adverbially (meaning "quite" or "completely"), does not agree with a feminine adjective when that adjective begins with a vowel.

Elle est toute petite.
Elle était tout étonnée.
Elles sont toutes petites.
Elles étaient tout étonnées.

POSSESSIVE ADJECTIVES

Although not generally used for personal description, parts of the body, and so forth, possessive adjectives are required when referring to someone else, or when beginning a sentence.

Mes mains sont sales.
J'ai mis le livre dans votre poche.
Vous avez vu leurs cheveux?
J'aime cette femme. Son visage est joli.
Ses bras sont brunis.
Son corps est maigre.
Il a pris mon chapeau.
Voilà vos gants.
Où est votre manteau?

For emphasis or clarity an extra prepositional phrase may be added.

C'est mon livre à moi.
Ce sont ses gants à elle.

4

PERSONAL PRONOUNS, DIRECT OBJECTS, COMMANDS

DIRECTIONS: Complete each of the following sentences by writing the appropriate pronoun on the numbered lines to the right.

1. _____ ont une grande maison. (they)

2. _____ êtes très intelligent. (you)

3. Je _____ vois tous les jours. (her)

4. _____ va souvent au cinéma. (she)

5. Nous _____ remercions. (you)

6. _____ es grande! (you)

7. _____ arrivent ce soir. (they, fem.)

8. _____ voyez-vous? (them)

9. Ils ne _____ donnent pas. (it, masc.)

10. Ne _____ voit-elle pas? (us)

11. _____ aimez-vous? (her)

12. _____ voilà! (I)

For each of the following sentences, write T (True) on the line at the right if it is correct and write F (False) if it is incorrect.

13. Je les aime.

14. L'attendez-vous?

15. Je la n'aime pas.

16. Leur regarde-t-elle?

17. Vous ne m'aidez pas.

18. La donnez à Jean!

19. Ne le voulez-vous pas?

20. Ne les aidez pas!

1	
2	
3	
4	
5	
6	
7	
8	
9	
10	
11	
12	
13	
14	
15	
16	
17	
18	
19	
20	

BASIC FACTS

PERSONAL PRONOUNS, DIRECT OBJECTS

SING.	PLUR.
me	nous
te, vous	vous
le, la, l'	les

The pronoun forms *nous* and *vous* are the same as the subject forms. *Te,* like the subject form *tu,* is a familiar form of *vous;* normally *tu* and *te* should only be used when addressing members of one's own family, intimate friends, or fellow students.

Direct object pronouns always immediately precede the main verb whether the sentence is affirmative, negative, interrogative, negative-interrogative, or negative imperative.

Je le vois.
Je ne le vois pas.
Le voyez-vous?
Ne le voyez-vous pas?
Ne le voyez pas!

The only exception to this rule is the positive imperative (command) when the pronoun object follows the verb and is linked to it by a hyphen.

Regardez-le!   Regardez-la!
Regardez-les!   Regardez-nous!

NOTE: The only pronoun forms that change in these circumstances are *me* (which becomes *moi*) and *te* (which becomes *toi*).

Regardez-moi!   Mets-toi là!

Like nouns that indicate people, nouns referring to things also have the direct object pronoun forms *le, la, l',* and *les,* and these are used according to gender and number in the usual way.

Paul donne son livre à sa soeur.
Paul le donne à sa soeur.

(Continued on page 16)

ADDITIONAL INFORMATION

OTHER USES OF THE DIRECT OBJECT PRONOUN *le*

English often omits the word "it" when referring to an implied idea or a concept, but in French this must be included in the sentence in the form of *le*. This word is invariable since it does not refer to a specific noun.

Il est malade. Oui, je le sais.
Qu'a-t-il fait? Dites-le-moi!
Comme il vous l'a déjà dit, il est français.
Comme vous le savez sans doute, il est malade.

Le also sometimes indicates the English word "so."

Vous me l'avez dit hier.
Le croyez-vous?
S'il le désire, j'accepte son offre.

VERBS INTRANSITIVE IN ENGLISH, BUT TRANSITIVE IN FRENCH

In English, some verbs take an indirect object and thus require a preposition such as "at," "for," or "to." Some of these verbs are transitive in French, and so take a direct object instead.

attendre	chercher	demander
écouter	payer	regarder

Vous l'attendez depuis longtemps?
Je le cherche, mais je ne le trouve pas.
Nous ne le demandons jamais.
Il écoute la radio dans sa chambre.
Il a payé son auto.
Je les regarde avec plaisir.

DIRECT OBJECTS WITH INFINITIVES

When the direct object is truly governed by the main verb it precedes that verb.

Je les vois sortir.
Ils ne vous entendent pas chanter.
Les regardez-vous danser?
Elle les fait venir.
Je les envoie chercher.
Vous les écoutez crier?
Il la laisse faire?

The same procedure is followed with an imperative plus an infinitive.

Regardez-les danser!
Ecoutez-la chanter!
Entendez-les s'amuser!

(Continued on page 16)

EXPLANATIONS

1. ***Ils*** *ont une grande maison. Ils* is the masculine subject pronoun form for "they."

2. ***Vous*** *êtes très intelligent. Vous* is the pronoun form for *êtes*. It can mean one person or several.

3. *Je **la** vois tous les jours. La* is the object pronoun "her" or "it" (fem.).

4. ***Elle*** *va souvent au cinéma. Elle* is the subject pronoun for "she."

5. *Nous **vous** remercions. Vous* is the same for both subject and object.

6. ***Tu*** *es grande! Tu* is the pronoun form for *es*.

7. ***Elles*** *arrivent ce soir. Elles* is the feminine subject pronoun "they."

8. ***Les*** *voyez-vous? Les* is the object pronoun "them."

9. *Ils ne **le** donnent pas. Le* is the object pronoun for "it" (masc.) or "him."

10. *Ne **nous** voit-elle pas? Nous* is the same for both subject and object.

11. ***L'****aimez-vous? L'* replaces *le* or *la* before a vowel or silent *h*.

12. ***Me*** *voilà!* In French *me* is the object of *voilà*.

13. *Je les aime.* Both subject and object normally precede the verb in French.

14. *L'attendez-vous?* The object precedes the verb in a question.

15. *Je ne l'aime pas* is the correct form. The object must normally directly precede the verb.

16. *Les regarde-t-elle?* would be correct. *Regarder* means "to look at" and takes a direct object.

17. *Vous ne m'aidez pas.* The object directly precedes the verb according to rule.

18. *Donnez-la à Jean* is the correct form. In a positive command the object must follow the verb.

19. *Ne le voulez-vous pas?* The object precedes the verb, as usual.

20. *Ne les aidez pas.* In a negative command the object precedes the verb.

Answers	
Ils	1
Vous	2
la	3
Elle	4
vous	5
Tu	6
Elles	7
Les	8
le	9
nous	10
L'	11
Me	12
T	13
T	14
F	15
F	16
T	17
F	18
T	19
T	20

Cherche-t-elle la petite fille?
La cherche-t-elle?
N'aimez-vous pas le cinéma?
Ne l'aimez-vous pas?
Je n'envoie pas les livres à Pierre.
Je ne les envoie pas à Pierre.

THE IMPERATIVE

Normally the 2nd person plural form of the verb is used, without its subject pronoun *vous,* for a command.

Venez ici!   *Cherchez-le!*
Donnez-le à Jean.   *Apportez-la!*

In the negative, the same verb form is employed, but if there is a pronoun object it belongs in the normal place for pronoun objects—before the verb.

Ne venez pas!   *Ne le cherchez pas!*
Ne les donnez pas à Jean!
Ne l'apportez pas!

The familiar 2nd person singular form of the verb may be used for an imperative if the circumstances call for it.

Viens ici!   *Prends-le!*
Mets ton manteau! *Attends!*

In the 1st conjugation, however, the imperative form of the 2nd person singular drops the *-s.*

Cherche-le!   *Donne-le à Jean!*
Regarde-moi!   *Ecoute!*

Notice that the irregular imperative of *aller* is *va,* except before *y.*

Va là!   *Vas-y!*

Fais-le venir!
Vois-le sauter!
Envoyez-les chercher!
Laissez-le étudier!

But in the negative imperative the direct object pronoun is again placed before the verb.

Ne les regardez pas danser!
Ne l'écoutez pas chanter!
Ne le fais pas venir!
Ne le vois pas sauter!
Ne les envoyez pas chercher!
Ne le laissez pas étudier!

If the infinitive governs the direct object, however, the latter must directly precede the infinitive.

Je peux le faire.
Il ne veut pas me voir.
Vous insistez à le dire?
Ne préfèrent-ils pas vous accompagner?
Elle aime les entendre.
Nous aimons mieux l'écouter.

In the case of an imperative plus an infinitive the same rules apply.

Insistez à le dire!
Veuillez me voir!
N'insistez pas à le dire!

THE 3RD PERSON IMPERATIVE

This form of the imperative, preceded sometimes in English by the word "may" or "let," implies an unexpressed wish for someone else; therefore, in French it requires the present tense of the subjunctive mood, sometimes without *que.*

Vive le Président!
Qu'ils viennent!
Qu'elle refuse!
Qu'il réussisse!

THE 1ST PERSON PLURAL IMPERATIVE

This is formed from the present indicative verb, omitting the pronoun *nous,* and means "let us."

Allons au cinéma!
Donnons de l'argent à ce pauvre homme.

5

ADVERBS

DIRECTIONS: Complete each sentence with the appropriate form of the adverb, and write your answers on the numbered lines to the right.

1. *Il marche* _____. (*lent*)

2. *Elle parle* _____. (*gentil*)

3. *Vous travaillez* _____ *que votre frère.* (*bon*)

4. *Je chante* _____. (*constant*)

5. *Il l'aime* _____. (*énorme*)

6. *Il étudie* _____. (*mauvais*)

7. *Nous travaillons* _____ *que les autres.* (*beaucoup*)

8. *Il se couche* _____. (*tard*)

9. *Vous parlez* _____. (*bref*)

10. *Il était* _____ *grand!* (*tel*)

11. *Vous y allez* _____? (*vrai*)

12. *Il court* _____. (*vite*)

1 _____

2 _____

3 _____

4 _____

5 _____

6 _____

7 _____

8 _____

9 _____

10 _____

11 _____

12 _____

BASIC FACTS

FORMATION OF ADVERBS

Adverbs are usually formed from the feminine adjective plus the ending *-ment.*

lent	*lente*	*lentement*
heureux	*heureuse*	*heureusement*

If the masculine adjective already ends in a vowel, however, the feminine *-e* is not required.

vrai	*vraiment*
absolu	*absolument*

The most common exceptions and irregularities are the following:

bref	*brève*	*brièvement*
gai	*gaie*	*gaiement*
gentil	*gentille*	*gentiment*

Notice the following examples:

aveugle	*aveugle*	*aveuglément*
commun	*commune*	*communément*
confus	*confuse*	*confusément*
énorme	*énorme*	*énormément*
obscur	*obscure*	*obscurément*
précis	*précise*	*précisément*
profond	*profonde*	*profondément*

ADVERBS OF MANNER AND EJACULATIONS

Que means "what!" or "how!"

Que de patience il faut avoir!
Qu'elle est jolie!

Comme can be translated as "how!" "since," "as if," or "like."

Comme elle est polie!
Comme il fait froid, nous rentrons.
Il parle comme pour dire adieu.
Il est intelligent comme son père.

Comment means "how?" or "what!"

Comment allez-vous?
Comment! Vous avez fini?

ADVERBS OF QUANTITY

Most adverbs and other expressions of quantity take *de* before an object.

(*Continued on page 20*)

ADDITIONAL INFORMATION

Unlike English usage, a French adverb does not separate a verb from its subject. The best and usual place for a French adverb is directly after the verb unit whether in the affirmative, interrogative, or negative construction.

Il le fait volontiers.
Parlent-elles toujours?
Nous ne jouons pas fréquemment au tennis.

Sometimes the construction of the sentence is improved by putting a long adverb at the beginning or at the end.

Maintenant je vais vous raconter une histoire.
Nous n'allons pas le voir immédiatement.

If there are two adverbs, they may be placed together or separately.

Ne voyagent-ils pas toujours ensemble?
Malheureusement je ne l'ai pas vu après.

Adverbial expressions of place usually follow the verb and precede the object.

Il sort du tiroir une belle cravate.

Short adverbs usually precede an infinitive; others follow it.

Il ne faut pas trop demander.
Pour bien apprendre il faut bien étudier.
Je dois le demander immédiatement.

ADVERBIAL EXPRESSIONS

En retard means "late" in the sense of after an appointed time, not necessarily late in the day.

Vous êtes en retard!
Le train est en retard.

Notice the following expressions with *fois:*

à la fois	at the same time
maintes fois	many times, often
parfois	occasionally
plusieurs fois	several times
quelquefois	sometimes

The following are idioms using *temps:*

à temps	in time, on time
de temps à autre	now and again
de temps en temps	from time to time
en même temps	at the same time, together

(*Continued on page 20*)

EXPLANATIONS

1. *Il marche* **lentement.** This is typical of the regularly formed adverb, which takes the feminine form of the adjective and adds the ending -*ment,* which is equivalent to the English "-ly."

2. *Elle parle* **gentiment.** *Gentil* (feminine *gentille*) is irregular in its adverbial form, perhaps because the ending -*ille* has no strong consonant sound.

3. *Vous travaillez* **mieux** *que votre frère.* As in English, forms for "better," "worse," etc. are irregular.

4. *Je chante* **constamment.** This is an irregular form, somewhat typical of adjectives ending in -*ant.*

5. *Il l'aime* **énormément.** This also is an irregular development and is found in some adverbial forms.

6. *Il étudie* **mal.** *Mal* is another irregular form, typical of those expressing degrees of "good," "bad," etc.

7. *Nous travaillons* **plus** *que les autres. Plus* already means "more," so no other word is needed.

8. *Il se couche* **tard.** Adverbs of time, place, manner, and quantity are not formed in the same way as other adverbs; they usually consist of one word.

9. *Vous parlez* **brièvement.** Although the feminine form of the adjective *bref* is *brève,* the adverb is *brièvement* and the noun is *brièveté.*

10. *Il était* **tellement** *grand. Tellement* is the adverbial form accompanying an adjective.

11. *Vous y allez* **vraiment?** Masculine adjectives ending in a vowel usually take the adverbial ending without the feminine -*e.*

12. *Il court* **vite.** *Vite* is an exceptional adverbial form, just as "fast" is in English; it also means "quickly."

Answers

lentement	1
gentiment	2
mieux	3
constamment	4
énormément	5
mal	6
plus	7
tard	8
brièvement	9
tellement	10
vraiment	11
vite	12

Il a beaucoup de courage.
Elle a tant d'amis.
Nous avons trop de choses à faire.
J'ai tant de travail à finir.
Avez-vous assez de timbres?
Ont-ils autant de livres que vous?

Plus and *moins* are also followed by *de* when meaning quantity, and by *que* in comparisons.

Il a plus d'argent que de sens.
Elle a moins de trois mille dollars.
J'ai plus de temps que vous.
Ils mangent moins que nous.

ADVERBS OF PLACE

Où may mean "where," "in which," "on which," or even "when."

C'est la maison où je suis né.
Le moment où vous êtes arrivé...

Notice the following expressions:

quelque part	somewhere
nulle part	nowhere
partout	everywhere
de toutes parts	on all sides
d'autre part	on the other hand

ADVERBS OF TIME

Auparavant means "before" in the strict sense of time; *après* means "after."

Quelque temps auparavant...
Peu de temps après...

Tôt is "early"; *tard* is "late."

Je suis arrivé très tôt.
Il vient trop tôt.
Il rentre tard.
Vous partez si tôt?

Notice the following expressions:

aussitôt	at once, immediately
bientôt	soon

Tantôt... tantôt means "sometimes . . . sometimes."

Tantôt il neige, tantôt il gèle.

Enfin means "finally," "at last," or "in short."

Enfin, le voilà!   Enfin, il est parti.

Bien also emphasizes adjectives or verbs, or serves as an adjective instead of *bon* or *joli.*

Bien entendu!   Je le pense bien!
Vous avez bien reçu son cadeau?
Il y a bien deux cents pages dans ce livre.
Ma chambre est bien chaude.
Ce chapeau est très bien.

Peu used with an adjective has the effect of minimizing or contradicting the original meaning.

C'est peu probable!
L'eau est peu profonde.

Notice the following expressions:

à peu près	approximately, nearly
peu à peu	little by little

Do not confuse *peu* (few, little) with *un peu* (a little).

J'ai très peu de livres.
Donnez-moi un peu de lait, s'il vous plaît.

Davantage, meaning "more" or "more so," is not followed by *de* or *que,* and usually ends the sentence.

Il est studieux, mais Paul l'est davantage.
Vous êtes fatigué. Reposez-vous davantage.

Adverbial expressions sometimes replace the simple adverb or are employed because there is no adverb.

à haute voix	aloud
à tâtons	gropingly, by touch
avec succès	successfully
d'une voix basse	in a low tone
d'une façon désagréable	disagreeably
par accident	accidentally
par hasard	by chance

ADJECTIVES USED ADVERBIALLY

When adjectives are used adverbially, they are invariable.

aller [tout] droit	to go straight [ahead]
s'arrêter net	to stop dead
couper court	to cut short
coûter cher	to be expensive, to cost a lot
frapper juste	to strike home, to strike true
parler haut (ou bas)	to speak loudly (or low)
sentir bon (ou mauvais)	to smell good (or bad)
tenir bon	to hold (stand) firm
travailler ferme	to work steadily (hard)
voir clair	to see clearly

6 COMPARATIVES, SUPERLATIVES; *C'EST* AND *IL EST*

DIRECTIONS: Select the appropriate adjective or adverb listed below for each of the following sentences, and write your answers on the lines to the right.

1. *Il le fait _____ que son frère.*   *belles*

2. *Votre soeur est plus _____ que vous.*   *pis*

3. *J'attends ma soeur. Elle est _____.*   *mieux*

4. *Sont-ils les plus _____?*   *meilleure*

5. *Je suis _____ fatigué que vous.*   *moindre*

6. *Jean est mauvais, mais Paul est _____.*   *intelligents*

7. *Elles sont les plus _____ de toutes.*   *moins*

8. *C'est mal! C'est encore _____!*   *petite*

9. *Laquelle est la _____?*   *pire*

10. *Cela n'a pas la _____ importance.*   *en retard*

Complete the following sentences with either *c'est* or *il est* as required.

11. *Il fait beau aujourd'hui. _____ bien!*

12. *_____ intéressant de les voir.*

13. *_____ facile à faire.*

14. *Votre frère? _____ insupportable!*

15. *M. Dupont? _____ un Français.*

16. *_____ là où ils sont morts?*

17. *_____ bien de noter tous les détails.*

18. *_____ dix heures et demie.*

19. *_____ temps de partir.*

20. *Qu'est-ce que _____?*

1 _____
2 _____
3 _____
4 _____
5 _____
6 _____
7 _____
8 _____
9 _____
10 _____
11 _____
12 _____
13 _____
14 _____
15 _____
16 _____
17 _____
18 _____
19 _____
20 _____

BASIC FACTS

COMPARATIVES

In making the regular comparative form of an adjective or adverb in French, *plus* indicates the idea of increase (English examples: "pretti*er*," "more beautiful") and *moins* the idea of decrease (English: "less pretty").

Ma soeur est plus âgée que moi.
Il est moins grand que son frère.
Je lis plus facilement maintenant.
Il parle moins couramment que nous.

Notice the forms *plus mauvais* and *pire*; both mean "worse," but the former applies to a material idea whereas the latter refers to less concrete things.

Cette route est bien plus mauvaise!
La crainte est pire que la vérité.

SUPERLATIVES

To make the regular superlative form of an adjective in French, *le plus, la plus, les plus* (or *le moins, la moins, les moins*) are used. Notice the repetition of the article if the superlative follows the noun.

le garçon le plus intelligent
la plus grande idée
les enfants les plus misérables
le moins actif des frères
la chose la plus importante
les plus petites fleurs

Observe the forms *le plus petit*, etc. and *le moindre*, etc. The former means "smallest" (in size) and the latter means "slightest" or "least considerable."

C'est le plus petit.
C'est la moindre des choses.
Quels fruits sont les plus petits?

The superlative may also be employed with a possessive adjective. It occupies the same place as the simple adjective: if the adjective precedes the noun, so does its comparative form; if

(Continued on page 24)

ADDITIONAL INFORMATION

COMPARATIVES

Notice the expressions *de plus en plus* (more and more), *plus ... plus.* (the more . . . the more), and *moins... moins* (the less . . . the less).

Elle devient de plus en plus difficile.
Il travaille de plus en plus.
Plus j'essaie, plus je me sens encouragé.
Moins il étudie, moins il apprend.

Latin, which largely constitutes the basis of French and the other Romance languages (Italian, Spanish, Portuguese, and Romanian), had special forms for comparative adjectives and adverbs. Comparative adjectival endings were *-ior* (masc. and fem.), *-ius* (neuter). Neuter forms were later dropped entirely or became incorporated usually with the masculine form. English derived its *-er* and *-ior* comparative endings from the latter. French abandoned nearly all these endings in favor of *plus* and *moins*.

	LATIN		FRENCH	
	MASC.	FEM.	MASC.	FEM.
SING.	melior	melior	meilleur	meilleure
PLUR.	meliores	meliores	meilleurs	meilleures

The Latin ending for a comparative adverb was *-ius*, which is found in French only in rare forms.

LATIN	FRENCH
melius	mieux

SUPERLATIVES

The Classical Latin forms for the superlative adjective were *-issimus* (masc.), *-issima* (fem.), and *-issimum* (neuter). As usual, the neuter was later dropped, and none of these forms exists in modern French. The Classical Latin superlative adverb form usually ended in *-me* or *-issime*, but this did not develop into modern French.

C'est

C'est and its plural *ce sont* are required with a modified noun or a pronoun.

C'est une idée!
Est-ce un enfant intelligent?
C'est le comble!
Ce n'est pas la meilleure façon de le faire.
Ce sont mes amis.

Qui est là?	*C'est moi.*
C'est toi.	*C'est lui.*
C'est elle.	*C'est nous.*
C'est vous?	

(Continued on page 24)

EXPLANATIONS

1. *Il le fait **mieux** que son frère.* The comparative adverb tells how he did it.

2. *Votre soeur est plus **petite** que vous.* Only a simple feminine adjective is needed.

3. *J'attends ma soeur. Elle est **en retard.*** "Waiting" implies the idea of the sister's lateness.

4. *Sont-ils les plus **intelligents?*** The plural adjective completes the superlative.

5. *Je suis **moins** fatigué que vous.* The adverb completes the comparative.

6. *Jean est mauvais, mais Paul est **pire.*** The comparative adjective "worse" has an irregular form.

7. *Elles sont les plus **belles** de toutes.* The adjective completes the superlative.

8. *C'est mal! C'est encore **pis!*** The adverb "worse" is irregular in form.

9. *Laquelle est la **meilleure?*** The feminine singular superlative is needed.

10. *Cela n'a pas la **moindre** importance.* The superlative "slightest" is irregular.

11. *Il fait beau aujourd'hui. **C'est** bien!* C'est refers back to a statement already made.

12. ***Il est** intéressant de les voir.* The impersonal phrase *il est* introduces a new idea.

13. ***C'est** facile à faire.* C'est is used with an adjective followed by *à* and an infinitive.

14. *Votre frère? **Il est** insupportable.* Il est is required with an adjective alone describing a person.

15. *M. Dupont? **C'est** un Français.* C'est is needed with a modified noun.

16. ***C'est** là où ils sont morts?* Là indicates a place (noun), so *c'est* is required.

17. ***Il est** bien de noter tous le détails.* Il est again introduces a new idea.

18. ***Il est** dix heures et demie.* Time of day always requires *il est*.

19. ***Il est** temps de partir.* A new idea is introduced by *il est*.

20. *Qu'est-ce que **c'est?*** The answer will be a noun, so *c'est* is used.

Answers

mieux	1
petite	2
en retard	3
intelligents	4
moins	5
pire	6
belles	7
pis	8
meilleure	9
moindre	10
C'est	11
Il est	12
C'est	13
Il est	14
C'est	15
C'est	16
Il est	17
Il est	18
Il est	19
c'est	20

it normally follows, so does its comparative form, whether regular or irregular.

sa plus grande ambition
son camarade le plus intime
c'est le meilleur film français

To make the regular superlative form of an adverb, *le plus* and *le moins* are used. Notice that the article remains invariable for the adverb, although it may combine with a preposition.

C'est lui qui écrit le mieux.
Charles réussit le plus facilement.
Allez le voir le plus vite possible.
Il viendra demain au plus tard.

Observe the use of *de* to mean "in."

C'est le plus petit de la classe.

C'est, Il Est

It is often difficult for students to decide which of these expressions to use, yet, as usual in French, there are some basic rules that cover most cases. Perhaps it is best to remember that *ce* literally means "that" rather than "it." *C'est* is used in a simple exclamation referring to an idea or a statement.

C'est bien!
C'est vrai!
C'est curieux!

It also appears in a question of definition and in its reply.

Qu'est-ce que c'est?
C'est un chat.

Observe that for the 3rd person plural the plural *ce sont* is necessary.

Ce sont eux!

C'est and *ce sont* can be translated into the English "Are you the one(s) who?" "He is the one who," etc. The verb ending must agree with the pronoun used, unlike the English "You are the one who has . . ."

C'est vous qui avez fait cela?
Est-ce lui qui vous l'a dit?
C'est nous qui avons envoyé la lettre.
Ce sont elles qui ont répondu.

In an impersonal phrase with an adjective, *c'est* refers to some idea or statement already known and is followed by *à* before an infinitive.

Vous allez jouer du piano? C'est difficile à faire.
La guerre? C'est terrible à voir.

Il Est

Il est, elle est, ils sont, and *elles sont* are required with an unmodified noun (generally expressing occupation, nationality, group, or religion).

Il est français.
Elle est catholique.
Ils sont étudiants.

Il est is used for an impersonal phrase with an adjective to introduce a statement, fact, or idea not already mentioned, and is followed by *de* before an infinitive, or by *que* with a conjugated verb.

Il est difficile de le comprendre.
Il n'est pas facile de voir comment il le fait.
Il est certain qu'elle arrivera demain.
Est-il possible qu'ils viennent?

7

INDIRECT OBJECTS; *y* AND *en*

DIRECTIONS: Complete each of the following sentences by writing the appropriate pronoun on the numbered lines to the right.

1. *Il _____ donne un cadeau.* (her)

2. *_____ allez-vous?* (to it)

3. *Je ne vais pas _____ écrire.* (to him)

4. *Nous _____ sommes de retour.* (from it)

5. *Ne _____ avez-vous pas écrit?* (to me)

6. *_____ a-t-il?* (any)

7. *Je suis sûr qu'il _____ est.* (at it)

8. *_____ ont-ils envoyé une carte?* (to us)

9. *Elle va _____ répondre.* (them)

10. *Dites- _____ de venir.* (him)

For each of the following sentences, write T (True) on the line to the right if it is correct and write F (False) if it is incorrect.

11. *Y va-t-il?*

12. *Nous allons lui le donner.*

13. *Il n'en y a pas.*

14. *Donnez-les-moi, s'il vous plaît.*

15. *Elle va lui les envoyer.*

16. *Ne vous l'a-t-elle pas dit?*

17. *En avez-vous reçu?*

18. *Il les a dit la vérité.*

19. *Voulez-vous me l'expliquer?*

20. *Je ne l'ai pas téléphoné.*

1	
2	
3	
4	
5	
6	
7	
8	
9	
10	
11	
12	
13	
14	
15	
16	
17	
18	
19	
20	

BASIC FACTS

INDIRECT OBJECTS

SUBJECT	DIRECT OBJECT	INDIRECT OBJECT
je	me	me
tu	te	te
il	le	lui
elle	la	lui
nous	nous	nous
vous	vous	vous
ils	les	leur
elles	les	leur

Observe the similarities in the forms of the 1st and 2nd persons singular and plural. Notice also that the same form *lui* means "to him" or "to her," and *leur* means "to them" (masc. or fem.).

Y means "to it," "at it," "in it," "on it," or "there."

> *Il y va.*
> *Elle y est.*
> *Sont-ils sur la table? Ils y sont.*
> *Est-il dans le tiroir? Il y est.*

En means "of it," "of them," "from it," "any," or "some."

> *J'en ai.*
> *Elle en a trois.*
> *En revenez-vous?*
> *Il n'en a pas.*

THE PLACE OF INDIRECT OBJECTS

Like other pronoun objects, indirect objects precede the verb or an infinitive except in the positive imperative, when they follow.

> *Je lui ai dit de venir.*
> *Allez-vous leur donner ces livres?*
> *Donnez-moi votre chapeau!*

THE ORDER OF PRONOUN OBJECTS

If in an ordinary statement (whether affirmative, interrogative, negative, or negative-interrogative) there is more than one pronoun object, the following order must be observed:

(*Continued on page 28*)

ADDITIONAL INFORMATION

Some verbs, transitive in English, require the preposition *à* in French before a person object, and therefore take an indirect pronoun object: *assister à, déplaire à, désobéir à, insister à, nuire à, obéir à, plaire à, renoncer à, résister à, ressembler à, succéder à, survivre à.*

> *Jean déplaît à ses camarades. Il leur déplaît.*
> *Elle désobéit souvent à sa mère. Elle lui désobéit souvent.*
> *Cela va nuire aux enfants. Cela va leur nuire.*
> *Obéissez-vous à votre frère? Lui obéissez-vous?*
> *Cela plaît à mes amis. Cela leur plaît.*

Although English often omits the preposition, French verbs of communication need the preposition *à* before the person object, since it is really the indirect object: *demander à, dire à, prêter à, répondre à, téléphoner à.*

> *Demandez à Jean de venir. Demandez-lui de venir.*
> *Il dit à sa mère d'attendre. Il lui dit d'attendre.*
> *Voulez-vous prêter le livre à Marie? Voulez-vous lui prêter le livre?*
> *Elle ne répond pas à son père. Elle ne lui répond pas.*
> *Je vais téléphoner à ma soeur. Je vais lui téléphoner.*

Certain other verbs in French also require the preposition *à* and an indirect pronoun object, where English would use the preposition "from": *acheter à, arracher à, cacher à, emprunter à, prendre à, voler à,* etc.

> *Je vais lui emprunter son livre.*
> *L'agent leur a pris les passeports*
> *Il m'a volé tout mon argent.*

This seems a curious usage, but it is easily explained by the fact that in Classical Latin *ad* meant "to" or "at," and *ab* meant "from" or "away from." As often happened in the development of Latin into French, the final consonant of both *ad* and *ab* was dropped, leaving *a*, which became *à* in modern French—the accent being added to distinguish it from *a*, meaning "has."

PERSONAL PRONOUNS WITH REFLEXIVE VERBS

The 1st and 2nd person pronouns in the singular and plural have the same forms for the direct objects of reflexive verbs. Often these verbs are not expressed as such in English.

Je me lave.	I wash [myself].
Tu te lèves.	You get [yourself] up.
Nous nous couchons.	We go [put ourselves] to bed.
Vous vous réveillez.	You wake [yourself] up.

(*Continued on page 28*)

EXPLANATIONS

1. *Il **lui** donne un cadeau.* "Her" really means "to her," so the indirect object is required.

2. ***Y** allez-vous?* The pronoun *y* means "to it" or "there."

3. *Je ne vais pas **lui** écrire. Lui* means both "to him" and "to her."

4. *Nous **en** sommes de retour. En* means "of it" or "from it."

5. *Ne **m'**avez-vous pas écrit? Me* before the verb means "me" or "to me."

6. ***En** a-t-il?* As a pronoun *en* also means "any."

7. *Je suis sûr qu'il **y** est. Y* also means "at it" or "there."

8. ***Nous** ont-ils envoyé une carte? Nous* means "us" or "to us."

9. *Elle va **leur** répondre. Répondre* needs an indirect object—"to them."

10. *Dites-**lui** de venir. Dire* requires an indirect personal object.

11. ***Y** va-t-il?* is correct. *Y* (meaning "to it" or "there") correctly precedes the verb.

12. When there are two 3rd person object pronouns, *le* (direct object) should precede *lui* (indirect object). The sentence should read: *Nous allons **le lui** donner.*

13. *Y* always precedes *en*. The sentence should read: *Il n'**y en** a pas.*

14. *Donnez-**les-moi**, s'il vous plaît.* This is correct. Following an imperative, the direct object precedes the indirect.

15. *Les* (direct object) should precede *lui* (indirect object). The sentence should read: *Elle va **les lui** envoyer.*

16. *Ne **vous l'**a-t-elle pas dit?* When there are two objects in different persons, *vous* (2nd person) correctly precedes *l'* (3rd person).

17. ***En** avez-vous reçu? En* correctly precedes the auxiliary verb.

18. *Dire* needs an indirect personal object —*leur*. The sentence should read: *Il **leur** a dit la vérité.*

19. *Voulez-vous **me** l'expliquer?* When there are two objects in different persons, *me* (1st person) correctly precedes *l'* (3rd person).

20. *Téléphoner* requires an indirect personal object—*lui*. The sentence should read: *Je ne **lui** ai pas téléphoné.*

Answers

lui	1
Y	2
lui	3
en	4
m'	5
En	6
y	7
Nous	8
leur	9
lui	10
T	11
F	12
F	13
T	14
F	15
T	16
T	17
F	18
T	19
F	20

1, 2, 3
direct, indirect
y, en

This means that a 1st or 2nd person pronoun precedes a 3rd, and both precede the verb or infinitive.

> *Je ne vous les donne pas.*
> *Il me le répète.*
> *Vont-ils nous les vendre?*

However, if both pronouns are 3rd person, the direct object must precede the indirect.

> *Elle le lui dit.*
> *Allons-nous les leur donner?*
> *Ne le leur avez-vous pas donné?*

Y and *en* follow all other pronoun objects, and *y* precedes *en*.

> *Les y voyez-vous?*   *Il y en a.*
> *Il leur en a donné.*

With the positive imperative form of the verb, all pronoun objects must follow as usual, but the order is different. Regardless of the person, the direct object precedes the indirect.

> *Donnez-le-moi, s'il vous plaît.*
> *Répétez-les-lui!*

In the negative form of the imperative, the pronoun objects precede the verb and follow the normal rules.

> *Ne me le donnez pas, s'il vous plaît.*
> *Ne les lui répétez pas!*

With an adverb, the usual rules are observed whenever possible.

> *Les y voyez-vous souvent?*
> *Ne me les donnez pas maintenant!*
> *Répétez-les-lui vite!*
> *Je ne le leur explique pas trop.*

Since the pronoun object must always be expressed, the usual rules of construction are observed.

> *Je me lève et je m'habille.*
> *Il ne se presse pas.*
> *Vous reposez-vous?*
> *Ne vous lavez-vous pas?*
> *Levez-vous!*   *Dépêchez-vous!*
> *Ne vous levez pas!*   *Ne vous dépêchez pas!*

Sometimes a verb that is not normally reflexive may become so in French.

> *Les portes du musée s'ouvrent à dix heures.*
> *L'autobus s'arrête à notre porte.*
> *Les enfants se réunissent le jeudi.*

Other French reflexive verbs express an English passive.

> *La bibliothèque se trouve à droite.*
> *Cela ne se fait pas.*
> *Les souvenirs se vendent partout.*
> *Je m'étonne.*
> *Il se trompe; le livre n'est pas là.*

When a verb (reflexive or not) with one *personal* pronoun is used with a second personal pronoun, it is customary (unlike normal French usage) to place the second pronoun separately after the verb and to add the preposition *à*.

> *Ne vous a-t-il pas présenté à elle?*
> *Je me confie à lui.*
> *Il ne s'adresse pas à moi.*

y AND *là*

Là also means "there," but it is not a pronoun object. It may be used instead of *y* for emphasis or when it stands without a verb.

> *Je l'ai mis là.*
> *Où l'avez-vous vu? Là!*

THE PREPOSITION *en*

Do not confuse the pronoun object with the preposition, usually meaning "in."

> *Ils sont allés en France, en été.*

En with the present participle also means "in," "while," or "by."

> *En parlant, on apprend à parler.*

8   COMPOUND PAST TENSE WITH *AVOIR*

DIRECTIONS: Select the appropriate form of the past participle, and write your answers (a, b, c, d, or e) on the numbered lines to the right.

1. *J'ai* _____ *les livres à Jean.*
   a *donnée* b *vendu* c *finis*
   d *lus* e *écrits*

2. *Je la lui ai* _____.
   a *vendu* b *écrit* c *lu*
   d *envoyée* e *envoyés*

3. *Ne les avez-vous pas* _____?
   a *vus* b *lu* c *finie*
   d *donné* e *écrit*

4. *Il ne l'a pas* _____.
   a *fais* b *fis* c *fait*
   d *faits* e *fit*

5. *Ont-ils* _____ *Marie?*
   a *vus* b *vue* c *vu*
   d *écrit* e *écrite*

6. *Nous avons* _____ *sa lettre.*
   a *reçut* b *recevra* c *écrite*
   d *reçue* e *reçu*

7. *Avez-vous* _____ *les lettres à la poste?*
   a *met* b *mis* c *mets*
   d *mises* e *mise*

8. *Je l'ai* _____.
   a *craint* b *crainte* c *crains*
   d *craints* e *craintes*

9. *Les a-t-il* _____?
   a *conduis* b *conduisis*
   c *conduit* d *conduits*
   e *conduite*

10. *Elle les a* _____.
    a *tint* b *tins* c *tenu*
    d *tenue* e *tenus*

11. *Voilà la photo que Pierre a* _____ *hier.*
    a *prendra* b *pris* c *prise*
    d *prévu* e *prévue*

12. *Il n'a pas* _____ *longtemps.*
    a *vive* b *vécu* c *vivra*
    d *vit* e *vis*

1	_____
2	_____
3	_____
4	_____
5	_____
6	_____
7	_____
8	_____
9	_____
10	_____
11	_____
12	_____

BASIC FACTS

PAST PARTICIPLES

donner—donné	*finir—fini*
vendre—vendu	*vouloir—voulu*
recevoir—reçu	

Verbs of the 1st conjugation (ending in -*er*) are the most numerous and the most regular. Verbs of the 2nd conjugation (ending in -*ir*) are generally regular, but some have a past participle ending in -*u* or -*ert*.

courir—couru	*couvrir—couvert*
tenir—tenu	*offrir—offert*
venir—venu	*souffrir—souffert*
vêtir—vêtu	

BUT: *mourir—mort*
   conquérir—conquis

Verbs of the 3rd conjugation (ending in -*re*) are apt to have an irregular past participle. Some end regularly in -*u* but contract or change the stem.

connaître—connu	*résoudre—résolu*
moudre—moulu	*vivre—vécu*

Some of them have a past participle ending in -*i* and some in -*is*.

nuire—nui	*mettre—mis*
rire—ri	*prendre—pris*
suffire—suffi	
suivre—suivi	

BUT: *naître—né*

Many of these participles end in -*t*.

conduire—conduit	*écrire—écrit*
craindre—craint	*faire—fait*
cuire—cuit	*frire—frit*
dire—dit	*traire—trait*

NOTE: Many verbs ending in -*aindre* and -*eindre* have a past participle like that of *craindre*. Verbs of the 4th conjugation (ending in -*oir*) regularly have a past participle ending in -*u,* but a number of them contract the stem.

   avoir—eu
   devoir—dû (fem. *due*)

(*Continued on page 32*)

ADDITIONAL INFORMATION

USES OF THE COMPOUND PAST TENSE

The *passé composé* is so called because it is composed of two parts—the auxiliary (normally *avoir*) and the past participle of the verb of action. It indicates one single action completed in the past.

Je l'ai vu hier.
Il a commencé à travailler ce matin.
Nous avons passé trois mois à Paris.

This tense has other English meanings.

J'en ai donné.	I have given some.
Vous l'avez dit.	You have said it.
Ont-ils fini?	Have they finished?
N'a-t-il pas réussi?	Hasn't he succeeded?

It can also be translated by the word "did."

L'avons-nous fini?	Did we finish it?
Tu l'as fait!	You did it!
Si, elle l'a dit!	Yes, she did say it!
Avez-vous cherché?	Did you search?

Observe the use of *si* to replace *oui* when used as a denial, or for refuting a doubt.

The compound past may also indicate a limited number of completed actions, but usually not habitual or often repeated acts.

Il l'a fait trois fois.
Vous l'avez répété à mon frère.

Normally the auxiliary and the past participle are not separated, except by a negative.

Elle n'a pas voulu le faire.

Most adverbs follow both parts of the tense.

Je l'ai vu constamment.
Vous l'avez vu hier?
Elle l'a dit gentiment.

However, some short adverbs may appear between the auxiliary and the past participle.

Nous l'avons souvent dit.
L'a-t-il déjà fait?

THE PRONOUN OBJECT *en*

Although a preceding direct object (noun or pronoun) requires the agreement of the past participle, the direct pronoun object *en* (meaning "some" or "of them") does not affect the past participle.

(*Continued on page 32*)

EXPLANATIONS

1. *J'ai **vendu** les livres à Jean. Vendu* is the regular past participle of *vendre* and is the only appropriate form to use here since a past participle with *avoir* does not normally vary.

2. *Je la lui ai **envoyée.*** The regular past participle of *envoyer* requires an additional *e* here since the direct object pronoun *la* precedes the auxiliary verb *avoir,* and the past participle must agree with it.

3. *Ne les avez-vous pas **vus?*** The regular past participle of *voir* requires an *s* added here because of the preceding direct object pronoun *les,* which is presumed to be masculine unless known to be feminine.

4. *Il ne l'a pas **fait.** Faire,* like most verbs with an infinitive ending in -*re,* has an irregular past participle. These irregular past participles should be carefully learned.

5. *Ont-ils **vu** Marie?* Although Marie is feminine, there is no direct object pronoun preceding the auxiliary verb; therefore, the regular past participle of *voir* does not change.

6. *Nous avons **reçu** sa lettre.* Verbs with infinitives ending in -*oir* are quite irregular. The cedilla is necessary for a soft sound of *c* before *a, o,* or *u.*

7. *Avez-vous **mis** les lettres à la poste? Mettre* has an irregular past participle form. Because the direct object follows, *mis* does not change here.

8. *Je l'ai **craint.** Craindre* also has an irregular past participle. The preceding direct object pronoun is presumed to be masculine.

9. *Les a-t-il **conduits?** Conduire* has an irregular past participle, and it needs an *s* added here to agree with *les.*

10. *Elle les a **tenus.** Tenir* has an irregular past participle ending in *u.* An *s* is required here to agree with *les.*

11. *Voilà la photo que Pierre a **prise** hier.* The irregular past participle of *prendre* needs an *e* here to agree with the preceding direct object *photo.*

12. *Il n'a pas **vécu** longtemps. Vivre* has a very irregular past participle.

Answers	
b	1
d	2
a	3
c	4
c	5
e	6
b	7
a	8
d	9
e	10
c	11
b	12

mouvoir—mû (fem. *mue*)
pleuvoir—plu
pouvoir—pu
recevoir—reçu
savoir—su
BUT: *(s') asseoir—assis*

The verbs *avoir* and *être* are also irregular.

avoir—eu   *être—été*

Remember that all compound verbs based on any of these infinitives have the same forms.

venir—venu	*revenir—revenu*
dire—dit	*redire—redit*
voir—vu	*revoir—revu*

AGREEMENT OF PAST PARTICIPLES

The past participle of a verb conjugated with *avoir* does not change.

J'ai vendu mon auto.
Avez-vous acheté des gants?
Il a reçu trois cadeaux.

If, however, a direct object (noun or pronoun) *precedes* the verb, the past participle must agree with it. A pronoun object is considered to be masculine unless it is known to be feminine.

Les lui avez-vous donnés?
Voici les cartes que j'ai achetées.
Marie? Je l'ai vue ce matin.

But if the object preceding the verb is indirect, the past participle does not change.

Marie? Je lui ai écrit hier.

Avez-vous acheté des timbres? Oui, j'en ai acheté vingt.
Leur a-t-il donné des billets pour le cinéma? Oui, il leur en a donné.

PAST PARTICIPLES USED AS ADJECTIVES

This use is a logical extension of the agreement of the past participle with a preceding direct object. The past participle may appear alone as an adjective.

Vues d'ici, les montagnes sont magnifiques.
Construite au moyen âge, la cathédrale est énorme.
Délivrés de leurs souffrances, ils ont commencé à vivre.
La représentation finie, les genes ont quitté la salle.

PAST PARTICIPLES USED FOR OTHER EXPRESSIONS

Sometimes a French past participle is translated as an English present participle. However, the French participle may really be more accurate since the actual gesture has already been performed. "Kneeling" really means "having knelt" or "in a kneeling *position*" (rather than an action); "sitting" more accurately means "having sat" or "in a sitting position"; and so forth.

Agenouillée près de son lit, elle a prié pour lui.
Confortablement assis dans un fauteuil, il fume sa pipe.
Couchés dans leurs lits, ils ont commencé à dormir.
Je l'ai vue, étendue sur l'herbe.
Penchés sur elle, deux hommes ont essayé de la ranimer.
Suspendu par une corde, un tableau décore le mur.

Sometimes English uses a past participle in this same way.

Ejected from her home, the poor woman sobbed bitterly.
Unfairly robbed of her heritage, the girl had to find a job.
Praised by all, he heard their cheers.

"TO LOOK," "SEEM"

The expression *avoir l'air* is employed with an adjective or with a past participle used as an adjective. The adjective or past participle usually agrees with the person or thing described.

Elle a l'air gaie.
Ils ont l'air fatigués.
Cette dame a l'air française.
Elles ont l'air confidentes.

But if the stress is on the look alone, the adjective or past participle agrees with *air*.

Sa mère a l'air craintif.
Ces savants ont l'air bête.

COMPOUND PAST WITH *ÊTRE*, PERFECT INFINITIVE, PRESENT PARTICIPLE

DIRECTIONS: Complete each sentence with the appropriate past participle of the given verb, and write your answers on the lines to the right.

1. *Elle s'est* _____ *(lever).*

2. *N'y sont-ils pas* _____ *(aller)?*

3. *Vous êtes tous* _____ *(arriver)?*

4. *Marie et Jean sont* _____ *(venir).*

5. *Est-il* _____ *(descendre)?*

6. *Elle s'est* _____ *(acheter) des gants.*

7. *Nous sommes* _____ *(tomber) dans la rue.*

8. *Vous êtes-vous* _____ *(écrire) chaque jour?*

9. *Est-elle* _____ *(sortir)?*

10. *Elles se sont* _____ *(rencontrer) hier.*

For each of the following sentences, write T (True) on the line to the right if it is correct and write F (False) if it is incorrect.

11. *Ils s'en sont allés.*

12. *Je m'en suis souvenu.*

13. *Ils se sont parlés.*

14. *Elle s'est regardée dans la glace.*

15. *Nous nous sommes moqué d'eux.*

16. *Elles se sont retourné.*

17. *Ils se sont demandé si c'était vrai.*

1	
2	
3	
4	
5	
6	
7	
8	
9	
10	
11	
12	
13	
14	
15	
16	
17	

BASIC FACTS	ADDITIONAL INFORMATION

BASIC FACTS

VERBS CONJUGATED WITH *Être*

aller	*venir*
arriver	*partir*
entrer	*sortir*
monter	*descendre*
naître	*mourir*
rester, tomber, retourner	

These intransitive verbs—almost all verbs of motion—are conjugated with *être* instead of *avoir,* and the past participle refers to and agrees with the subject.

> *Elle est partie hier.*
> *Ils sont arrivés.*
> *Je suis né* (or *née*) *à Paris.*
> *Vous êtes venu* (*venue, venus,* etc.).

All compounds of these verbs are also conjugated with *être: rentrer, remonter, renaître, repartir, ressortir, retomber, revenir.*

REFLEXIVE VERBS

All reflexive verbs are also conjugated with *être: s'en aller, s'écrier, s'emparer, s'enfuir, s'évanouir, se moquer, se réfugier, se repentir, se retourner, se souvenir,* etc.

Revenir means "to return" (to come back to where the speaker is), *retourner* means "to return" to a place away from the speaker, and *se retourner* means "to turn around."

> *Elle s'en est souvenue.*
> *Ils se sont retournés.*
> *Vous vous êtes toutes évanouies?*
> *Elles se sont repenties.*

Most of these verbs are followed by *de* plus the object.

> *Il s'est réfugié de ses ennemis.*
> *Elles se sont enfuies de lui.*
> *Vous vous moquez de moi.*

(Continued on page 36)

ADDITIONAL INFORMATION

OTHER VERBS THAT MAY CHANGE THEIR AUXILIARY

A number of French verbs that are apparently intransitive and thus conjugated with *être* may be used with a direct object and conjugated with *avoir.*

> *Il est monté à sa chambre.*
> *Il a monté les bagages.*
> *Êtes-vous descendu?*
> *Avez-vous descendu la valise?*
> *Elle n'est pas sortie.*
> *Elle n'a pas sorti les photos.*
> *Ne sont-ils pas rentrés?*
> *N'ont-ils pas rentré les chaises?*

THE PERFECT INFINITIVE

The perfect infinitive is formed with either *avoir* or *être* plus the past participle, according to the usage rules for verbs with *avoir* or *être.* Notice, however, that English does not normally use a past infinitive.

> *Après avoir fini son travail, il est sorti.*
> After finishing his work, he went out.
> *Après être arrivé, Jean a dormi.*
> After arriving, John slept.
> *Il est inutile d'avoir fait cela.*
> It's useless to have done that.
> *Je suis content d'y être retourné.*
> I am glad to have gone back there.

Observe that the past participle with the infinitive *être* agrees with the subject in the usual way.

> *Après être arrivés, nous sommes allés au cinéma.*
> *Être revenues pour rien, elles le regrettent.*

It is often possible to use a substitute for the past infinitive in French. A noun, sometimes with a past participle, is a good alternative.

> *Son travail fini, il est sorti.*
> *Après son arrivée, Jean a dormi.*
> *Je regrette mon retour.*

VARIABLE USES OF THE PAST PARTICIPLE WITH TWO VERBS

A number of English verbs are expressed by two verbs in French.

entendre dire	to hear (someone say)
envoyer chercher	to send for, to send to fetch
faire cuire	to cook (something)
faire savoir	to inform
faire suivre	to forward (letters, etc.)

(Continued on page 36)

EXPLANATIONS

1. *Elle s'est* **levée.** In a reflexive verb, if the preceding pronoun object is the *direct object* of the verb, the past participle agrees with it. In this example *s'* means "herself" and is the direct object of the action.

2. *N'y sont-ils pas* **allés?** The past participle agrees with the *subject* of a non-reflexive verb conjugated with *être.*

3. *Vous êtes tous* **arrivés?** *Arrivés* agrees with the masculine plural subject *vous.*

4. *Marie et Jean sont* **venus.** *Venus* agrees with the plural mixed gender subject.

5. *Est-il* **descendu?** The past participle agrees with the subject *il.*

6. *Elle s'est* **acheté** *des gants.* In contrast to Question·1 (above), *s'* is *not* the direct object of the verb here; therefore, the past participle does not agree with it. In this example, *s'* means "for herself."

7. *Nous sommes* **tombés** *dans la rue.* The past participle agrees with the plural subject.

8. *Vous êtes-vous* **écrit** *chaque jour?* Like Question 6, the object pronoun *vous* is not the direct object, so the past participle does not agree.

9. *Est-elle* **sortie?** The past participle agrees with the subject *elle.*

10. *Elles se sont* **rencontrées** *hier. Rencontrées* agrees with the preceding direct object *se.*

11. *Ils* **s'en** *sont* **allés.** Like Questions 1 and 10, *allés* in its reflexive form agrees with the preceding direct object *s'.*

12. *Je m'en suis* **souvenu.** *Souvenu* is correct, assuming that the preceding direct object *m'* is masculine.

13. The sentence should read: *Ils se sont* **parlé.** *Se* in this example is an indirect object, meaning "to each other."

14. *Elle* **s'est** **regardée** *dans la glace.* The past participle correctly agrees with the direct object *s'.*

15. *Nous* **nous** *sommes* **moqués** *d'eux.* Since this verb is only used reflexively, the past participle agrees.

16. The sentence should read: *Elles* **se** *sont* **retournées.** *Se retourner* means "to turn around," so *se* is the direct object and *retournées* agrees.

17. *Ils* **se** *sont* **demandé** *si c'était vrai. Se* is indirect since *demander* needs *à* before a personal object.

Answers	
levée	1
allés	2
arrivés	3
venus	4
descendu	5
acheté	6
tombés	7
écrit	8
sortie	9
rencontrées	10
T	11
T	12
F	13
T	14
F	15
F	16
T	17

VERBS THAT MAY BECOME REFLEXIVE

Some verbs normally conjugated with *avoir* may become reflexive if the action is done to the subject. In that case they are conjugated with *être*.

Ils se sont regardés.
Nous nous sommes cherchés.
Elles se sont rencontrés.

Some verbs may be reflexive or non-reflexive according to need, and they take the appropriate auxiliary.

Je me suis lavé(e).
J'ai lavé la voiture.
Elle ne s'est pas levée.
Elle n'a pas levé la chaise.
Nous nous sommes habillés.
Nous avons habillé les enfants.

NON-AGREEMENT OF PAST PARTICIPLE

A number of verbs may become reflexive, but because the reflexive pronoun object is not a direct object, the past participle does *not* agree with it. In these cases the reflexive pronoun object means "to each other," "for each other," "to himself," "for herself," etc.

Ils se sont donné des cadeaux.
Elle s'est acheté une robe.
Nous ne nous sommes pas écrit.
Marie s'est demandé si...
Nous nous sommes dit que...
Elles se sont parlé hier.

NOTE: *se demander* also means "to wonder."

Cadeaux is the direct object of the first example, *robe* of the second. In the other examples the direct object is not expressed.

faire venir	to send for
laisser tomber	to drop
vouloir dire	to mean

Depending upon the meaning, the past participle **may** or may not agree with the object. Generally the past participle will agree with its own preceding direct object. But if the direct object is controlled by the infinitive itself, the past participle does not agree.

La femme qu'il a envoyée chercher Paul est sa soeur.
The woman whom he sent to fetch Paul is his sister.

Femme is the direct object of *a envoyée*.

La femme qu'il a envoyé chercher est sa soeur.
The woman whom he sent for is his sister.

Femme is *not* the direct object here since he sent someone else to fetch her.

Even if the infinitive is understood but not expressed, the past participle does not agree.

Nous avons fait toutes les tâches que nous avons pu [faire].

If the preceding direct object *le* or *l'* represents an idea rather than the noun or pronoun that began the sentence, then the past participle does not agree.

Ils étaient paresseux et elle l'a cru.

The past participle of some verbs only agrees with the preceding noun or pronoun direct object when the sense is figurative and not literal.

courir	*coûter*	*régner*
valoir	*vivre*	

Les risques qu'elle a courus ne valaient pas la peine.
Les kilomètres qu'il a couru sont impressionnants.

THE PRESENT PARTICIPLE

The present participle for all verbs is formed by adding the ending *-ant* to the stem of the 1st person plural of the present indicative tense. It is the equivalent of the English form "-ing."

(nous) **donn**ons	*donnant*	giving
(nous) **finiss**ons	*finissant*	finishing
(nous) **vend**ons	*vendant*	selling
(nous) **voy**ons	*voyant*	seeing

However, it must be remembered that the present participle has only a limited use in French, and it never appears as part of a main verb or after any preposition except *en*.

Donnant la main à chacun, il leur a dit bonsoir.
Shaking hands . . .
En parlant, on apprend à parler.
By (in, while, through) speaking . . .

10

SELF-TEST

DIRECTIONS: Select the appropriate negative listed below for each of the following sentences, and write your answers on the lines to the right.

1. *Elle ne parle _____. (not)*   *aucune*

2. *Ne l'avez-vous _____ vu? (not at all)*   *jamais*

3. *Ils n'ont _____ fait.*   *ni... ni*

4. *N'y allez _____!*   *aucun*

5. *Vous n'avez _____ idée du problème.*   *pas*

6. *Je ne les ai _____ vus.*   *personne*

7. *Nous n'avons vu _____.*   *plus*

8. *Elles n'ont parlé _____ de cela.*   *point*

9. *Il n'a fait _____ effort.*   *rien*

10. *Vous n'avez vu _____ Paul _____*   *que*
    Marie?

For each of the following sentences, write T (True) on the line to the right if it is correct and write F (False) if it is incorrect.

11. *Personne ne m'a vu.*   16. *Elle n'a personne vu.*

12. *Je n'ai ni vu mon père ni ma mère.* 17. *Nous n'avons fait absolument rien.*

13. *Il n'a jamais rien dit.*   18. *Elles ont peur qu'il ne le lui donne.*

14. *N'y êtes-vous retourné plus?*   19. *Rien n'est pas arrivé.*

15. *Ils n'ont fait rien.*   20. *Je crains qu'elle ne me trouve pas ici.*

1
2
3
4
5
6
7
8
9
10
11
12
13
14
15
16
17
18
19
20

BASIC FACTS

ne... pas   *ne... point*
ne... plus   *ne... jamais*
ne... rien

With a simple tense, *ne* precedes the verb and the negative word follows it. Remember, however, that these are not double negatives. *Ne* means "not" or "no," and the other part of the negation has a positive sense: "no . . . more," "no . . . longer," "not . . . ever," "not . . . anything," etc.

> *Je ne le vois jamais.*
> *Il n'y est plus.*
> *Elles n'ont rien.*

Ne may appear with two negative words.

> *Il ne fait jamais rien.*
> *Je n'y vais jamais plus.*

Both parts of a negative precede a simple infinitive except *personne.*

> *Elle m'a dit de ne pas attendre.*
> *Je ne veux jamais plus l'entendre.*
> *Il parle de ne voir personne.*

Jamais, when used without the negative means "ever."

> *Avez-vous jamais vu ce garçon?*
> *Si jamais elle vient.*
> *Sans jamais parler, il est sorti.*

Rien may be used alone after *sans.*

> *Sans [jamais] rien dire...*

Notice that *plus, jamais, rien, aucun(e),* and *personne* may appear alone in a negative sense. *Aucun(e)* is an adjective and agrees with its noun.

> *Plus de joie, plus de bonheur!*
> *L'avez-vous jamais vu? Jamais!*
> *Qu'a-t-elle fait? Rien!*
> *N'écrivent-ils aucune lettre? Aucune!*
> *Qui est venu? Personne.*

In a compound tense most negatives keep their normal place before and after the main verb (the auxiliary).

(*Continued on page 40*)

ADDITIONAL INFORMATION

OMISSION OF *pas* AFTER CERTAIN VERBS

If the negative idea is not strong, *pas* may sometimes be omitted from the negative after *pouvoir, savoir, oser,* and *cesser. Pas* is never used with *je ne puis.*

> *Je ne puis dire cela.*
> *Il ne pouvait l'imaginer.*
> *Elle ne saurait l'expliquer.*
> *Je ne sais s'il viendra ou non.*
> *Les enfants n'osent lui désobéir.*
> *Ils ne cessaient de la regretter.*

THE USE OF *Non*

Non appearing alone may mean "not" as well as "no."

> *Non loin de leur maison il y a un bois.*
> *Non seulement Pierre mais Paul aussi l'a nié.*
> *C'est son frère, non son cousin, qui l'a dit.*
> *Je l'ai fait, mais non sans effort.*

Non used with *pas* indicates a stronger negative.

> *Ce sont ces amis, non pas ses parents, qui l'ont aidé.*

EXPRESSIONS WITH *pas*

Certain idioms employ *pas* alone in an adverbial expression. The phrase "not at all" may be rendered in several ways, even without *pas.*

> *L'avez-vous vu? Pas du tout.*
> *Vous a-t-elle écrit? Du tout.*
> *L'a-t-il rencontrée? Point du tout.*

Observe that as usual *point* has a stronger meaning than *pas.* An adverb may strengthen the word *pas.*

> *L'ont-ils fait? Absolument pas!*
> *Voulez-vous le faire? Certainement pas!*

Sometimes *ne* is included in such expressions as "not even."

> *Elle ne m'a même pas écrit.*

Notice the phrase meaning "not that I know [of]."

> *Est-il chez lui? Pas que je sache.*

Observe the use of *pas* in the idiom "not yet."

> *Sont-elles arrivées? Pas encore.*

Remember that *encore* only means "still" or "yet."

> *Y est-il encore? Je crois que oui.*
> *L'avez-vous fait? Pas encore.*

(*Continued on page 40*)

EXPLANATIONS

1. *Elle **ne** parle **pas.*** This is correct for a simple negative.

2. ***Ne** l'avez-vous **point** vu?* This is a stronger negative, and it precedes a past participle.

3. *Ils **n'ont rien** fait.* Normally the negative word precedes a past participle.

4. ***N'y** allez **plus!*** As usual the negative word follows the main verb.

5. *Vous **n'avez aucune** idée du problème.* The appropriate form of *aucun* precedes its noun.

6. *Je **ne** les ai **jamais** vus.* *Jamais* precedes the past participle.

7. *Nous **n'avons** vu **personne.*** *Personne* follows the past participle.

8. *Elles **n'ont** parlé **que** de cela.* *Que* follows the past participle.

9. *Il **n'a** fait **aucun** effort.* *Aucun* agrees with and precedes its noun.

10. *Vous **n'avez** vu **ni** Paul **ni** Marie?* *Ni* precedes both nouns.

11. ***Personne ne** m'a vu.* *Personne* may be used as the subject of a sentence.

12. *Ni* should precede the noun. The sentence should read: *Je **n'ai** vu **ni** mon père **ni** ma mère.*

13. *Il **n'a jamais rien** dit.* Even two negative words normally precede the past participle.

14. *Plus* should precede *retourné*. The sentence should read: ***N'y** êtes-vous **plus** retourné?*

15. This should be *Ils **n'ont rien** fait, rien* preceding *fait*.

16. *Personne* is an exception to the rule; it follows the past participle. The sentence should read: *Elle **n'a** vu **personne.***

17. *Nous **n'avons** fait absolument **rien.*** When emphasized by an adverb, *rien* may follow the past participle.

18. *Elles ont peur qu'il **ne** le lui donne.* *Ne* meaning "lest" instead of "not" is correctly used alone.

19. *Pas* is not used with another negative word. The sentence should read: ***Rien n'est** arrivé.*

20. *Je crains qu'elle **ne** me trouve **pas** ici.* *Ne* and *pas* are correctly used to mean "not."

Answers

pas	1
point	2
rien	3
plus	4
aucune	5
jamais	6
personne	7
que	8
aucun	9
ni... ni	10
T	11
F	12
T	13
F	14
F	15
F	16
T	17
T	18
F	19
T	20

Ils n'ont rien fait.
Elle n'est jamais venue.
Nous ne lui avons pas écrit.

But *ne... que, ne... aucun(e), ne... personne,* and *ne... ni... ni* are exceptions to this rule.

Je n'ai vu que Pierre.
Il n'a reçu aucune lettre.
Vous n'avez vu personne?
Elle n'a eu ni frère ni soeur.

Personne, aucun(e), rien, and *ni... ni* may begin a sentence.

Personne n'a répondu.
Aucun élève n'a réussi.
Rien n'est arrivé
Ni lui ni Marie n'a parlé.

Ne followed by one *ni* may be used when there are two verbs and one subject.

Je ne le juge ni le crois méchant.

Sans may also appear with one *ni.*

Sans argent ni amis...

Ni, when used alone with the expression *non plus,* means "nor . . . either" or "neither."

Il ne le dit pas. Ni moi non plus.

The negative expression *ni... ni* has a positive form, *ou... ou* (either . . . or).

Ni lui ni elle ne le fait.
Ou lui ou elle le fait.

Sometimes the second *ou* is followed by *bien,* meaning "or else."

Ou lui ou bien elle l'a fait.

Ou bien may also appear alone.

Il est là, ou bien il n'y est pas.

Occasionally *encore* may approximate the sense of "more."

En voulez-vous encore? Oui, s'il vous plaît.

To mean "again," the words *une fois* must be added to *encore.*

Voulez-vous le répéter encore une fois?

Notice that *merci* often has a negative meaning in reply to a question. It is positive only when one has received something and is saying thanks in return. In an affirmative reply *s'il vous plaît* is required.

Un peu de sucre? Merci.   (No, thank you).
Du lait? S'il vous plaît.
Voilà une lettre pour vous. Merci.

The Pleonastic *ne*

Frequently *ne* is used alone, not in a negative sense but to mean "lest," like the original Classical Latin word from which it originated. The negative *ne* is derived, like the negative French *non,* from the Classical Latin word *non. Ne* also appears after certain conjugations like *à moins que* and *avant que.* Besides meaning "lest" in expressions involving fear or precaution, *ne* is used after a comparative expression.

Je crains qu'elle n'arrive bientôt.
Il a peur que je ne le lui donne.
Prenez garde qu'ils ne vous trompent.
A moins que je ne le cherche, je le perdrai.
Avant qu'elle ne regarde sa chambre, nettoyez-la!
Ils sont plus riches que je ne pensais.
Son occupation est plus difficile qu'elle ne l'était.
Elle est moins intelligente qu'elle ne le semble.
Il a plus d'argent qu'il ne lui en faut.

Observe the use of *ne* in the following sentence after the meaning of "since."

Il y a longtemps que je ne lui ai écrit.

When the meaning is definitely negative, then of course *ne... pas* is used in the normal way.

Je crains qu'elle n'arrive pas bientôt.

Si Meaning "Yes"

For an affirmative answer contradicting a negative question or statement, *si* replaces *oui.* Normally *si* only means "if," "whether," or "so" (with an adjective or adverb).

Vous ne l'avez pas vu? Si, je l'ai vu.
Elle n'est pas intelligente. Si, elle l'est.

DIRECTIONS: Choose the appropriate relative adjective or pronoun, and write your answers (a, b, c, d, or e) on the lines to the right.

1. *Je ne sais pas* _____ *films vous avez vus.*
   a *quel*   b *quels*   c *lesquels*
   d *quelles*   e *lesquelles*

2. *Il me demande* _____ *sont ces dames.*
   a *à qui*   b *lesquelles*   c *quelles*
   d *qui*   e *dont*

3. *L'homme* _____ *nous avons pensé est son frère.*
   a *à qui*   b *de qui*   c *duquel*
   d *lequel*   e *quel*

4. *La seule date* _____ *je me rappelle, c'est 1789.*
   a *quelle*   b *laquelle*   c *quel*
   d *qui*   e *que*

5. *Le musée* _____ *je parle est le Louvre.*
   a *de qui*   b *de quoi*   c *duquel*
   d *de laquelle*   e *de quel*

6. *L'hôtel* _____ *ils se souviennent se trouve ici.*
   a *qui*   b *que*   c *de quoi*
   d *dont*   e *de quel*

7. *La dame, avec le frère* _____ *j'ai voyagé, est Mme Dupont.*
   a *à qui*   b *de qui*   c *quelle*
   d *qui*   e *duquel*

8. *Le professeur* _____ *je cherche est M. Smith.*
   a *que*   b *qui*   c *lequel*
   d *pour lequel*   e *dont*

9. *Le stylo avec* _____ *j'écris est terrible.*
   a *que*   b *quoi*   c *qui*
   d *quel*   e *lequel*

10. *Il a oublié dans* _____ *rue se trouve la gare.*
    a *laquelle*   b *quel*   c *quelle*
    d *lequel*   e *que*

11. *La façon* _____ *il le fait est formidable!*
    a *dans laquelle*   b *dont*
    c *de laquelle*   d *dans quoi*
    e *de que*

12. *Je ne peux décider* _____ *de ces robes je préfère.*
    a *quelle*   b *quelles*   c *que*
    d *quoi*   e *laquelle*

1 _____
2 _____
3 _____
4 _____
5 _____
6 _____
7 _____
8 _____
9 _____
10 _____
11 _____
12 _____

BASIC FACTS

RELATIVE ADJECTIVES

	MASC.	FEM.
SING.	quel	quelle
PLUR.	quels	quelles

Avez-vous décidé quel train arrive?
Il ne sait quelle décision prendre.
Avec quel enthousiasme elle parle!

The various forms of *quel* are used, like the English "what" or "which," directly with a noun, with or without a preposition. They may also appear in the same way in a question or an exclamation, without the indefinite article "a" as in English.

Quelle idée!   Quel homme est-ce?

PRONOUNS

	MASC.	FEM.
SING.	lequel	laquelle
PLUR.	lesquels	lesquelles

The definite article is added to and combined with the various forms of *quel* to make the pronoun; it stands alone but refers to a noun (person or thing) and must agree in gender with that noun.

Lequel de ces livres préférez-vous?
Auxquels des enfants parle-t-il?
La porte par laquelle on entre...

OTHER PRONOUNS

Qui means "who," or "whom" with a noun, preposition, or in a question.

L'homme qui l'a dit est mon père.
La dame avec qui je travaille...
Qui avez-vous vu?
A qui a-t-elle parlé?

Que replaces *qui* when it is a direct object alone or refers to a noun and means "what," "whom," or "that."

Qu'avez-vous dit?
L'homme que j'ai vu est Paul.

(Continued on page 44)

ADDITIONAL INFORMATION

INDEFINITE RELATIVE EXPRESSIONS

Certain current expressions in French indicate an indeterminate person in the sense of "whoever," "anyone at all," "it doesn't matter who," "somebody," "I don't know who," "anybody," etc.

Quiconque le fera sera admiré.
Celui qui l'a écrit est méprisable.
N'importe qui pourrait le faire.
N'importe quel endroit sera pareil.
Quel film voulez-vous voir? N'importe [lequel].
Où veut-il s'asseoir? N'importe où.
Je ne sais qui l'a fait.
Il l'a vu dans je ne sais quelle ville.
Elle y est arrivée je ne sais comment.

Similar expressions may indicate a thing.

Dites-lui n'importe quoi.
Nous pouvons faire n'importe quoi.
Elle raconte je ne sais quoi.
Quand je les vois j'éprouve un je ne sais quoi...

Dont

This useful word may replace the preposition *de* plus *qui*, *quoi*, or the various forms of *lequel*. *Dont* may mean "of whom," "of which," "whose," "about whom," etc.

Voilà la dame dont j'ai parlé.

Notice that when *dont* means "whose," the definite article must be used before the noun it governs, since *dont* strictly means "of whom" or "of which."

C'est l'homme dont la femme est française.

Remember also that the order of a French sentence changes when the noun governed by *dont* is the object of the next verb, not the subject.

C'est l'homme dont j'ai vu la femme hier.
It's the man whose wife I saw yesterday.

Dont is preferred with a verb that takes *de;* it must not be used with any other preposition.

Voilà les livres dont j'ai besoin.
C'est la photo dont je me souviens.
Le bureau dont je me sers est là.
C'est un homme dont je me méfie.
Les privilèges dont il abuse sont importants.
La femme avec le mari de qui je parle est ma soeur.

(Continued on page 44)

EXPLANATIONS

1. *Je ne sais pas **quels** films vous avez vus.* The noun *films* requires one of the relative adjective forms of quel—in this case the masculine plural form.

2. *Il me demande **qui** sont ces dames.* Here the relative pronoun is needed as the subject of the following verb. Notice the French word order; in English the verb would usually come last.

3. *L'homme **à qui** nous avons pensé est son frère.* The verb "to think about" takes *à* in French. *Qui* means "who" or "whom," and does not change after a preposition.

4. *La seule date **que** je me rappelle, c'est 1789.* Que is the direct object for "which," "that," or "whom." The verb *se rappeler* takes a direct object.

5. *Le musée **duquel** je parle est le Louvre.* The pronoun form *lequel,* referring back to the noun, is necessary here after a preposition, and the *le* combines with *à* or *de* in the usual way.

6. *L'hôtel **dont** ils se souviennent se trouve ici.* Dont may replace *de qui, duquel,* etc. and does so when the verb is followed by *de.*

7. *La dame, avec le frère **de qui** j'ai voyagé, est Mme Dupont.* In a phrase already containing one preposition *(avec), dont* may not be used.

8. *Le professeur **que** je cherche est M. Smith.* Chercher does not need a preposition in French, so the direct objective *que* is adequate.

9. *Le stylo avec **lequel** j'écris est terrible.* After a preposition, the pronoun form *lequel* is necessary.

10. *Il a oublié dans **quelle** rue se trouve la gare.* The noun *rue* requires one of the adjectival forms of *quel.*

11. *La façon **dont** il le fait est formidable!* In French the preposition "in" is not used with the words "way" or "manner." The shorter, simpler *dont* is preferred to *de laquelle.*

12. *Je ne peux décider **laquelle** de ces robes je préfère.* The pronoun form *laquelle,* referring to the noun *robes,* is necessary here.

Answers

b	1
d	2
a	3
e	4
c	5
d	6
b	7
a	8
e	9
c	10
b	11
e	12

Les dames qu'il a rencontrées...
Les étudiants qu'elle a cherchés...
Les choses qu'il a faites...

Quoi must replace *que* in a question, an exclamation, or following a preposition.

Quoi! Vous l'avez fini?
Avec quoi écrit-il?
J'oublie de quoi je parlais.
A quoi pensez-vous?

LONGER INTERROGATIVE FORMS

PERSON

SUBJECT	Qui est-ce qui?	Qui?
OBJECT	Qui est-ce que?	Qui?

Qui est-ce qui l'a fait?
Qui l'a fait?
Qui est-ce que vous avez vu?
Qui avez-vous vu?

Remember that *que* must be used for the direct object referring to a noun.

THING

SUBJECT	Qu'est-ce qui?	
OBJECT	Qu'est-ce que?	Que?

Qu'est-ce qui s'est passé?
Qu'est-ce que vous avez vu?
Qu'avez-vous vu?

Notice that there is only one subject form of "what" referring to a thing.

OTHER USES OF *qui*

Together with the preposition *à, qui* may indicate possession.

A qui est ce livre? A moi.

This use may also imply a sense of struggle as to who will win.

C'est à qui prendra le dessus.

Observe the idiomatic expression *à qui mieux mieux* (as to who can do something best).

Ils dansaient à qui mieux mieux.

Où

Instead of *dans* or *sur* plus the various forms of *lequel*, French usage often prefers the shorter word *où* to mean "in which," "on which," "where," or "when."

La maison dans laquelle il est né est très belle.
La maison où il est né est très belle.
La table sur laquelle j'ai mis les livres est solide.
La table où j'ai mis les livres est solide.
C'est au moment dans lequel je l'ai vu que j'ai compris.
C'est au moment où je l'ai vu que j'ai compris.

INDEFINITE RELATIVE PRONOUNS

SUBJECT	ce qui
OBJECT	ce que

Ce qui s'est passé est terrible.
Ce que je crains c'est le tonnerre.
Elle est sérieuse, et c'est ce qui m'étonne.

Ce qui and *ce que* literally mean "that which," and may also be translated as "what." Notice that when the prepositions *à* or *de* are involved, the French sentence literally becomes "that to which," "that about which," or "that of which."

Ce à quoi je pense, c'est à mon frère.
Ce dont j'ai besoin, c'est un bon repas.

OTHER USES OF *que*

Apart from *que* as the object in a question, it is sometimes used as an indefinite "what?"

Qu'est-elle devenue? Que se passe-t-il?
Que sont ces bruits?

Que also occurs in a phrase with *oui* or *non.*

Il dit que oui.　Elles disent que non.

This construction is derived directly from Latin, which also employed the relative *quod* in this way: *Dixit quod non.*

OTHER USES OF *quoi*

Quoi is sometimes used in questions, and *que* becomes *quoi* after a preposition.

De quoi parle-t-il?　Avec quoi pouvons-nous le faire?

Notice the idiomatic *à quoi bon.*

A quoi bon poser tant de questions?

Quoi is also required when there is no reference to a noun.

Je n'ai pas de quoi écrire.
Il n'a pas de quoi vivre.
Sur quoi, elle est partie.
Après quoi, il s'est assis.

12

IMPERFECT TENSE, DEMONSTRATIVE ADJECTIVES; *ON, DEPUIS, VENIR DE*

DIRECTIONS: For each of the following sentences, write T (True) on the line at the right if it is correct and write F (False) if it is incorrect.

1. *Hier je voyais mon ami.*

2. *Pendant qu'il lisait, elle écrivait.*

3. *Nous attendions Pierre quand vous êtes venu.*

4. *Soudain, il m'appelait.*

5. *Tout de suite ils le faisaient.*

6. *Tous les jours il allait la voir.*

7. *Vite, il partait.*

8. *Je vous attendais depuis trois heures.*

9. *La maison était vieille et jolie.*

10. *Quand il a été jeune il était intelligent.*

Complete each of the following sentences with the correct form of the demonstrative adjective: *ce, cet, cette,* or *ces.*

11. *Voyez-vous _____ homme?*

12. *_____ livres sont intéressants.*

13. *Qui est _____ dame?*

14. *_____ garçons ne sont pas aimables.*

15. *_____ arbre et _____ fleurs sont jolis.*

16. *Je n'ai pas vu _____ film.*

17. *Où sont _____ billets?*

18. *Nous n'aimons pas _____ espèce de concert.*

19. *_____ enfants! Qu'ils sont difficiles!*

20. *Voulez-vous voir _____ musée?*

1	
2	
3	
4	
5	
6	
7	
8	
9	
10	
11	
12	
13	
14	
15	
16	
17	
18	
19	
20	

BASIC FACTS

INFINITIVE **donn**er
PRESENT INDICATIVE nous **donn**ons
IMP. IND. je **donn**ais
      (I was giving, used to give, gave)
        tu **donn**ais
    il (elle) **donn**ait
      nous **donn**ions
      vous **donn**iez
  ils (elles) **donn**aient

The imperfect indicative is one of the most regular tenses in its formation. Take the stem of the 1st person plural of the present indicative tense of any French verb and add the endings -*ais*, -*ais*, -*ait*, -*ions*, -*iez*, -*aient*.

nous finissons	*je finissais,* etc.
nous venons	*je venais,* etc.
nous vendons	*je vendais,* etc.

The imperfect indicative tense in French indicates an action that is incomplete, indefinite, often repeated, or long continued. It is also required for descriptions in past time.

> *Il étudiait quand je suis entré.*
> *Il était temps de partir.*
> *Tous les jours il y allait.*
> *Pendant vingt ans il travaillait.*
> *Elle était jeune et jolie.*

In deciding when to use the imperfect instead of the compound past (if it is not clearly expressed in English), it is often helpful to see whether the sentence includes some adverb or expression indicating duration of time or frequency of action such as "often," "usually," "every day," "once a week," etc. If so, the imperfect is correct. Beware of the English use of the conditional "would" in the imperfect sense of repeated action; this requires the imperfect in French.

> *Chaque jour il allait voir son ami.*
> Each day he would go to see his friend.

(Continued on page 48)

ADDITIONAL INFORMATION

DURATION OF TIME

The present and imperfect indicative tenses in French may express duration of time. To indicate duration of time up to the present, *depuis* is used with the present indicative tense.

> *J'attends depuis une heure.*
> I have been waiting for an hour.
> *Depuis combien de temps habite-t-il ici?*
> [For] how long has he been living here?

Similarly, *depuis* together with the imperfect specifies duration of time in the past.

> *J'attendais depuis une heure.*
> I had been waiting for an hour.
> *Depuis combien de temps habitait-il ici?*
> [For] how long had he been living here?

Voilà and *il y a*, which are more emphatic than *depuis*, may also be employed in this way with the present and imperfect tenses. Observe the use of *que* and the difference in word order.

> *Voilà une heure que j'attends!*
> *Il y a une heure que j'attends.*

Remember that the question "how long?" may be asked with *il y a* but not with *voilà*.

> *Combien de temps y a-t-il que vous attendez?*

"TO HAVE JUST"

The same two tenses, the present and imperfect indicative, may appear in another idiomatic construction, *venir de*. In the present tense, it means "have just" or "has just," and *de* is followed in the normal way by an infinitive.

> *Il vient d'entrer dans l'hôtel.*
> *Nous venons d'arriver.*
> *Elles viennent de sortir.*
> *Je viens de le voir.*

In the last example notice that *de* and *le* do not contract since they are not connected in meaning. *Le* is controlled by the infinitive *voir*, and *de* belongs to the verb *viens*. The sentence can be translated literally as "I come from seeing him." Similarly, *venir de* with the imperfect indicative means "had just."

(Continued on page 48)

EXPLANATIONS

1. The imperfect tense is wrong for one complete action. The sentence should read: *Hier j'ai vu mon ami.*

2. *Pendant qu'il lisait, elle écrivait.* This sentence is correct because both actions were incomplete.

3. *Nous attendions Pierre quand vous êtes venu.* This is correct since the first action is incomplete and the second complete.

4. One complete action requires the compound past tense. The sentence should read: *Soudain, il m'a appelé.*

5. The compound past is necessary. The sentence should read: *Tout de suite ils l'ont fait.*

6. *Tous les jours il allait la voir.* This is correct because a repeated action requires the imperfect.

7. Since this is a complete action, the sentence should be in the compound past tense: *Vite, il est parti.*

8. *Je vous attendais depuis trois heures.* The imperfect is correct for duration of time with *depuis.*

9. *La maison était vieille et jolie.* The imperfect is necessary for a description in past time.

10. Since description requires the imperfect, the sentence should read: *Quand il était jeune il était intelligent.*

11. *Voyez-vous cet homme?* The masculine *cet* is needed before a silent *h.*

12. *Ces livres sont intéressants.* The plural form *ces* agrees with *livres.*

13. *Qui est cette dame?* A feminine singular noun requires *cette.*

14. *Ces garçons ne sont pas aimables. Ces* is the plural form, agreeing with *garçons.*

15. *Cet arbre et ces fleurs sont jolis. Cet* is needed before a vowel; *ces* agrees with *fleurs.*

16. *Je n'ai pas vu ce film.* The masculine singular *ce* is correct before a consonant.

17. *Où sont ces billets?* The plural *billets* requires the plural *ces.*

18. *Nous n'aimons pas cette espèce de concert.* The feminine singular *espèce* calls for *cette.*

19. *Ces enfants! Qu'ils sont difficiles! Ces* agrees with the plural *enfants.*

20. *Voulez-vous voir ce musée? Musée* is masculine singular and therefore needs *ce.*

Answers

F	1
T	2
T	3
F	4
F	5
T	6
F	7
T	8
T	9
F	10
cet	11
Ces	12
cette	13
Ces	14
Cet, ces	15
ce	16
ces	17
cette	18
Ces	19
ce	20

Notice that the imperfect may be used in a sentence with another imperfect, with a present participle, or with a compound past tense (the imperfect indicating what was already going on when the main action happened).

> *Il travaillait et j'étudiais.*
> *En le faisant, elle chantait.*
> *Nous lisions quand elle est entrée.*

DEMONSTRATIVE ADJECTIVES

	MASC.	FEM.
SING.	ce, cet	cette
PLUR.	ces	

Observe the masculine form *cet,* which is necessary before a masculine singular word beginning with a vowel or a mute *h.*

> *cet habit*   *cette enfant*
> *ce garçon*   *cette hache*
> *ces habits*   *ces enfants*
> *ces garçons*   *ces haches*

The various forms of *ce* may mean "this" or "that." To be more specific, *-ci* may be added to the noun to mean "this" (literally, "this . . . here") or *-là* to mean "that" (literally, "that . . . there").

> *J'aime ce bracelet-ci.*
> *Voyez-vous cet homme-là?*
> *Nous avons vu ces films-là.*

Notice that *-ci* and *-là* are invariable.

> *Il venait d'entrer dans l'hôtel.*
> *Nous venions d'arriver.*
> *Elles venaient de sortir.*
> *Je venais de le voir.*

These meanings may also be translated literally as "He was coming from (the action of) entering the hotel," etc. Do not try to translate the English "have just" or "had just" into French literally; the French word *juste* means something else.

THE INDEFINITE PRONOUN *On*

A most versatile little word, *on,* may mean "one," "someone," "people," "they" (indefinite, not specific), or even "we."

> *Ici on parle français.*
> *On m'a dit qu'il est français.*
> *On parle toujours trop.*
> *On vend des souvenirs près du musée.*
> *Qu'est-ce qu'on va faire aujourd'hui?*

However, if "they" is specific, *ils* (or *elles*) is required.

> *Où sont les enfants? Ils sont en ville.*

AVOIDING THE PASSIVE VOICE

In French the active voice is preferred over the passive because it is usually clearer, shorter, and simpler. Especially where the agent or doer of the action is not known, *on* is very helpful in replacing the subject and making the sentence active.

> *Ici on parle français.*   French is spoken here.
> *On dit qu'il est avocat.*   He is said to be a lawyer.

Another means of avoiding the passive is the reflexive pronoun *se.*

> *Cela ne se fait pas.*   That isn't done.
> *Les portes se ferment à midi.*   The doors are closed
> at noon.

Of course, if the doer of the action is known, the whole sentence may be recast in the active voice.

> *Jean a été écrasé par un autobus.*
> *Un autobus a écrasé Jean.*
> *Marie est aimée de ses amies.*
> *Ses amies aiment Marie.*

13 DEMONSTRATIVE PRONOUNS, FUTURE TENSE

DIRECTIONS: Select the appropriate demonstrative pronoun listed below for each of the following sentences, and write your answers on the numbered lines to the right.

1. *Le meilleur étudiant n'est pas celui-ci mais _____.*   *ceux-là*

2. *De ces deux robes j'aime mieux _____ que vous portez.*   *celui*

3. *Les garçons d'ici sont plus grands que _____ du sud.*   *celles qui*

4. *_____ -là est le train pour Paris.*   *celui-là*

5. *Il préfère mes idées à _____ de sa soeur.*   *celle-là*

6. *Lequel de ces livres préférez-vous? _____.*   *celle*

7. *Celle-ci? Oh non, _____ est meilleure.*   *ceux*

8. *_____ sont les seuls individus qui l'intéressent.*   *celui-ci*

9. *Elle préfère _____ sont plus intelligentes que celles-ci.*   *celle-ci*

10. *_____? Elle n'est pas du tout jolie.*   *celles*

For each of the following sentences, write T (True) on the line at the right if it is the correct use of the future tense and write F (False) if it is incorrect.

11. *Viendra-t-elle demain?*

12. *S'il arrivera, je le verrai.*

13. *Elle alla au théâtre ce soir.*

14. *Nous le faisons bientôt.*

15. *Je me demande s'il l'acceptera.*

16. *Vous le recevoir tout de suite.*

17. *Quand il arrivera, vous comprendrez.*

18. *Si elle l'écrit demain, vous l'aurez après-demain.*

19. *L'envoyaient-ils à Paris?*

20. *Il sera bientôt ici.*

1	
2	
3	
4	
5	
6	
7	
8	
9	
10	
11	
12	
13	
14	
15	
16	
17	
18	
19	
20	

BASIC FACTS

DEMONSTRATIVE PRONOUNS

	MASC.	FEM.
SING.	celui	celle
PLUR.	ceux	celles

These forms of the demonstrative pronoun, like other pronouns, replace a noun; they must agree in gender and number with the noun to which they refer. They cannot stand entirely alone, but must be followed by *qui* (subject), *que* (object), *de, -ci,* or *-là.*

Celui qui aime est heureux.
Celle que vous voyez est sa femme.
Les films? J'aime ceux de Dassin.
Voyez-vous ces robes? Celles-ci?
Quels livres a-t-il? Ceux-là.

Notice that these pronouns may occupy various positions in the sentence. These pronoun forms may also appear with prepositions or prepositional expressions.

Persons

Celui dont je parle est son mari.
Celle à qui je pense c'est Marie.

Things

Ceux dont je parle sont ici.
Ceux desquels je parle sont ici.
Celui auquel je pense est à lui.

INVARIABLE DEMONSTRATIVE PRONOUNS

Ceci usually means "this" (thing, idea, or phrase) and *cela* means "that" (thing, idea, or phrase). Because these pronouns refer to an intangible thing or idea, they are invariable.

Il a dit ceci: « A demain! »
Ecoutez ceci! C'est joli!
Cela ne sert à rien.

THE FUTURE INDICATIVE TENSE

The regular future indicative tense

(Continued on page 52)

ADDITIONAL INFORMATION

OTHER USES OF DEMONSTRATIVE PRONOUNS

The plural adjectives *tous* and *toutes* often appear with *ceux* and *celles.*

Tous ceux qui sont absents le regretteront.
Toutes celles dont il parle sont intelligentes.

When *-ci* and *-là* are both used in one sentence, *-ci* means "the latter" (the nearest or latest mentioned) and *-là* "the former" (the furthest or previously mentioned).

Voilà Pierre et Jean. Je préfère celui-ci à celui-là.
Des deux robes j'aime mieux celle-là à celle-ci.

OTHER USES OF INVARIABLE DEMONSTRATIVE PRONOUNS

Ceci also keeps the meaning of *ici* (here), in the sense that it frequently indicates something yet to come and still unsaid.

Ecrivez ceci, mes enfants: « Bonjour, Madame.»
Il m'a donné ceci. C'est une carte.

Cela, in contrast, often refers to something in the past or already mentioned.

Cela ne m'amuse pas.
Il a déjà dit cela plusieurs fois.

Cela is sometimes translated as the English "it," followed by *de* or *que.*

Cela m'amuse d'aller voir le marché.
Cela ne vous ennuie pas qu'il soit parti?

Remember that *ça* is the contracted form of *cela* and should only be used when speaking or when indicating speech in written form.

Ça va? Oui, merci, ça va bien.
Soudain, il a demandé « Qu'est-ce que c'est que ça?»
Oh, pardon, il y a une erreur! Ça ne fait rien, Monsieur.

Cela (or *ça*) may be followed by *ce* and the verb *être.*

Ça? Ce n'est rien.
Ça, c'est une chose curieuse.

THE FUTURE INDICATIVE TENSE

As in English, the French future tense indicates an event that is about to happen at some time in the future, and it has only the one meaning.

Il viendra nous voir ce soir.

(Continued on page 52)

EXPLANATIONS

1. *Le meilleur étudiant n'est pas celui-ci mais **celui-là**.* The comparison needs the same pronoun plus *-là*.

2. *De ces deux robes j'aime mieux **celle** que vous portez.* The feminine singular form refers to *robe*.

3. *Les garçons d'ici sont plus grands que **ceux** du sud.* The masculine plural noun requires *ceux* to agree.

4. ***Celui**-là est le train pour Paris.* Since *-là* is added, only *celui* is needed—to agree with *train*.

5. *Il préfère mes idées à **celles** de ma soeur.* The feminine plural *celles* is correct here.

6. *Lequel de ces livres préférez-vous? **Celui-ci**.* The masculine singular demonstrative pronoun is needed here.

7. *Celle-ci? Oh, non, **celle-là** est meilleure.* The form *celle-là* is required in the comparison with *celle-ci*.

8. ***Ceux-là** sont les seuls individus qui l'intéressent.* The masculine plural form agrees with the noun.

9. *Elle préfère **celles qui** sont plus intelligentes que celles-ci.* The feminine plural form must be used here.

10. ***Celle-ci?** Elle n'est pas du tout jolie.* The feminine singular pronoun is called for here.

11. ***Viendra-t-elle** demain?* The future tense of *venir* is irregular.

12. The sentence should read: *S'il **arrive**, je le verrai.* *Si* (meaning "if") cannot immediately precede the future tense. It must be used with the present tense if the other clause contains the future tense.

13. The sentence should read: *Elle **ira** au théâtre ce soir.* The future of *aller* is irregular.

14. Since the future of *faire* is irregular, the correct sentence would be: *Nous le **ferons** bientôt.*

15. *Je me demande s'il l'**acceptera**.* Contrary to Question 12, *si* (meaning "whether") does take the future tense.

16. The future of *recevoir* is irregular; the sentence should read: *Vous le **recevrez** tout de suite.*

17. *Quand il **arrivera**, vous **comprendrez**.* In French the future is required for future actions.

18. *Si elle l'**écrit** demain, vous l'**aurez** après-demain.* *Si* (meaning "if") calls for the present tense here.

19. Since the future of *envoyer* is irregular, the correct sentence would be: *L'en-**verront**-ils à Paris?*

20. *Il **sera** bientôt ici.* *Être* has an irregular future.

Answers	
celui-là	1
celle	2
ceux	3
Celui	4
celles	5
celui-ci	6
celle-là	7
Ceux-là	8
celles qui	9
Celle-ci	10
T	11
F	12
F	13
F	14
T	15
F	16
T	17
T	18
F	19
T	20

is formed by adding certain endings to the infinitive.

INFIN.	FUTURE
donner	je donner**ai**
	tu donner**as**
	il (elle) donner**a**
	nous donner**ons**
	vous donner**ez**
	ils (elles) donner**ont**
finir	je finir**ai,** etc.
vendre	je vendr**ai,** etc.

Observe that 3rd conjugation verbs drop the final -e of the infinitive before adding the future endings.

Verbs of the 4th conjugation are generally quite irregular in the future.

INFIN.	FUTURE
avoir	j'aurai, etc.
savoir	je saurai
voir	je verrai
pouvoir	je pourrai
falloir	il faudra
valoir	je vaudrai
vouloir	je voudrai
devoir	je devrai
recevoir	je recevrai
apercevoir	j'apercevrai
pleuvoir	il pleuvra
(s')asseoir	je(m')assiérai
BUT: pourvoir	je pourvoirai

Other irregular future forms are:

aller	j'irai
envoyer	j'enverrai
courir	je courrai
mourir	je mourrai
tenir	je tiendrai
venir	je viendrai
être	je serai
faire	je ferai
BUT: cueillir	je cueillerai

Compounds of these verbs are similar.

Quand arrivera-t-elle?
Jeudi prochain j'irai voir ce film.
Nous vous reverrons bientôt.
Vous rentrerez à temps, n'est-ce pas?

THE DOUBLE FUTURE IN FRENCH

Unlike English, French generally employs a future tense after such expressions of time as *quand, lorsque, dès que, aussitôt que,* etc., even though the sentence may already have one future tense.

Je le verrai quand il arrivera.
Aussitôt qu'elles seront chez nous, elles se reposeront.
Venez me voir dès que vous rentrerez.

THE IMMEDIATE FUTURE

However, if the action is to happen in the immediate future, French often prefers the present to the future tense, especially with the verb *aller.*

J'y vais tout à l'heure.
Vous allez la voir ce soir?
Il va nous conduire?

PROBABILITY

The future tense in French may also indicate probability, as in the English phrases "no doubt," "probably," "do you suppose?" etc.

Où est Jean? Il sera chez lui.
Vous cherchez Marie? Sera-t-elle en ville?
Pierre est parti. Il aura du travail à faire.

SPELLING CHANGES IN SOME VERBS

In French a word with a stressed *e* must generally have either a grave accent on it or a double consonant following it, unless the *e* is the final vowel.

le père, la mère, le frère, etc.
quelle, j'appelle   BUT: *quel, appel*
le réverbère, la prière
une étincelle, une pelle

Therefore, the spelling of certain verbs must be changed in the future tense because the *e* takes on a stress by adding another syllable—in this case the endings *-ai, -as, -a,* etc.

acheter	j'achète	j'achèterai
appeler	j'appelle	j'appellerai
céder	je cède	je cèderai
BUT: préférer	je préfère	je préférerai

14 GEOGRAPHICAL TERMS, SEASONS

DIRECTIONS: Choose the correct geographical form or seasonal expression, and write your answers (a, b, or c) on the lines to the right.

1. *Je vais* _____ *France.* (to)
   a *à la*   b *en*   c *à*

2. *Elles sont* _____ *Paris.* (in)
   a *au*   b *en*   c *à*

3. *La France est* _____ *Europe.* (in)
   a *dans l'*   b *en*   c *dans*

4. *Il est né* _____ *Etats-Unis.* (in the)
   a *aux*   b *dans les*   c *en*

5. *Elle va* _____ *Canada.* (to)
   a *à*   b *au*   c *à la*

6. *Tours se trouve* _____ *Touraine.* (in)
   a *à la*   b *en*   c *dans*

7. _____ *Asie il y a beaucoup de pays.* (in)
   a *En*   b *Dans*   c *Dans l'*

8. *Marseille se trouve* _____ *Provence.* (in)
   a *dans*   b *dans la*   c *en*

9. _____ *été il va au bord de la mer.* (in)
   a *Dans l'*   b *En*   c *A l'*

10. *Il fait froid* _____ *hiver.* (in)
    a *en*   b *dans le*   c *dans l'*

11. *Les feuilles tombent* _____ *automne.* (in)
    a *dans l'*   b *à l'*   c *en*

12. *Les oiseaux chantent* _____ *printemps.* (in)
    a *en*   b *au*   c *dans le*

1
2
3
4
5
6
7
8
9
10
11
12

BASIC FACTS

GEOGRAPHICAL TERMS

Cities

The names of most French cities are masculine.

Paris, Bordeaux, Lyon, Tours

However, if the name ends in *-e*, it is usually feminine.

Nice, Marseille

Foreign cities are generally masculine also, even when there is a French version of the name.

Lisbonne, Londres, Edimbourg

The preposition *à* before the name of a city may mean "at," "in," or "to."

Le train arrive à New York.
The train arrives at New York.
Paul est à Bordeaux.
Paul is in Bordeaux.
Ils vont à Nice.
They are going to Nice.

Countries

Countries whose names end in *-e* are feminine, except *le Mexique*. Feminine names require *en* without an article to mean "in" or "to"; otherwise the definite article remains.

Ils sont en Espagne.
They are in Spain.
Allez-vous en Belgique?
Are you going to Belgium?
Aimez-vous la France?
Do you like France?

Provinces or States

Similarly, names of provinces or states ending in *-e* are feminine and are used with *en* ("in" or "to"). *Le Nouveau-Mexique* is an exception.

Strasbourg se trouve en Alsace.
Strasbourg is [located] in Alsace.

(*Continued on page 56*)

ADDITIONAL INFORMATION

CITIES THAT TAKE AN ARTICLE

The names of some French cities take an article, the main ones being *Le Havre, Le Mans, Le Touquet*. When the definite article forms part of the name, the prepositions *à* and *de* must combine with it in the usual manner.

Nous allons au Havre.
Il vient du Mans.
Ils sont au Touquet.

Occasionally a foreign city has an article in French, usually because it is modified by an adjective. In these cases also the prepositions *à* and *de* combine with the article.

Je vais à la Nouvelle-Orléans.
Mon frère m'a envoyé une carte de la Nouvelle-Orléans.

COUNTRIES THAT ARE MASCULINE

The names of most countries that do not end in an *-e* are masculine. Some of the important ones are *le Danemark, le Portugal, le Canada, les Etats-Unis*, and *le Japon*; most countries in Central and South America are also masculine: *le Salvador, le Brésil, le Pérou, l'Uruguay*, etc.

Mes cousins sont au Canada.
Vous allez au Brésil?
Elles viennent du Portugal.
La capitale des Etats-Unis est Washington.

THE PREPOSITIONS *y* AND *en*

Y, meaning "to it" or "there," replaces a prepositional phrase with *à* or *en*.

Nous voyageons au Danemark. Nous y voyageons.
Madrid se trouve en Espagne. Madrid s'y trouve.
Allons en France! Allons-y!
Georges est aux Etats-Unis. Georges y est.

En, in the sense of "of it" or "from it," stands for a prepositional phrase with *de*.

Elle arrive de Russie. Elle en arrive.
Nous venons de Rouen. Nous en venons.

THE PREPOSITIONS *pour* AND *pendant*

The English preposition "for" must usually be translated as *pendant* when the meaning applies to time.

Nous sommes restés à Paris pendant deux semaines.
Pendant trois années j'ai étudié à la Sorbonne.

(*Continued on page 56*)

EXPLANATIONS

1. *Je vais **en** France*. The preposition *en* is used with the names of feminine countries to mean "to" or "in."

2. *Elles sont **à** Paris*. The preposition *à* expresses the meaning "to," "in," or "at" before the name of a city.

3. *La France est **en** Europe*. The names of the continents are all feminine in French; therefore, *en* is required to translate "to" or "in."

4. *Il est né **aux** Etats-Unis*. French usage demands *à* plus the definite article to translate "to" or "in" before the name of a masculine country.

5. *Elle va **au** Canada*. Even when the definite article is not expressed in English, *à* plus the definite article must be used in French with a masculine country.

6. *Tours se trouve **en** Touraine*. Touraine is a feminine province and thus takes the preposition *en*.

7. ***En** Asie il y a beaucoup de pays*. As in Question 3, *en* is correct here.

8. *Marseille se trouve **en** Provence*. *En* is needed with the name of a feminine province.

9. ***En** été il va au bord de la mer*. For most of the seasons, *en* is required to mean "in."

10. *Il fait froid **en** hiver*. *En* is again correct before the name of a season.

11. *Les feuilles tombent **en** automne*. *Automne* follows the rule of using *en*.

12. *Les oiseaux chantent **au** printemps*. *Printemps* is the exception to the rule that *en* is used before names of seasons; *au* is correct here.

Answers

b	1
c	2
b	3
a	4
b	5
b	6
a	7
c	8
b	9
a	10
c	11
b	12

Nous allons en Californie.
We are going to California.
La Lorraine est belle.
Lorraine is beautiful.

Continents

The names of all of the continents end in *-e* and are feminine in French. They, too, need the preposition *en* ("in" or "to").

La Chine est en Asie.
China is in Asia.
Jean va en Amérique.
John is going to America.
L'Australie est grande.
Australia is large.

THE PREPOSITION "FROM"

De (without an article) means "from" when used with the name of a city, country, province, state, or continent.

Ils sont de Dijon.
They are from Dijon.
Elle vient d'Angleterre.
She comes from England.
Ils arrivent de Bretagne.
They are arriving from Brittany.
Vous êtes parti de Floride?
You left from Florida?
Nous venons d'Afrique.
We come from Africa.

SEASONS

The French names of the seasons, are all masculine. The preposition *en* (in) is required with all of them except one.

le printemps (spring)	*au printemps*
l'été (summer)	*en été*
l'automne (autumn)	*en automne*
l'hiver (winter)	*en hiver*

Il était en Europe pendant six mois.
Pendant huit jours elle était malade.

The preposition *pour* only indicates future time.

Elle va à New York pour quatre semaines.
Vous serez ici pour cinq jours?
Il n'est pas là pour toujours!
Pour toute une semaine je vais m'amuser.

THE PREPOSITION *dans*

Dans may sometimes replace *à* in the geographical sense if it really means within a limited space, such as a city.

Dans Paris il y a beaucoup de cinémas.
Ils vont passer leur temps dans Avignon.

Dans is required when a continent or a feminine country is modified by an adjective, adjectival expression, and/or article.

En France il y a beaucoup d'étudiants.
Dans la France moderne la politique est très importante.
Il va en Amérique.
Il va dans l'Amérique du Sud.
BUT: *Il va en Sud-Amérique.*

De USED WITH OR WITHOUT AN ARTICLE

If the sense is adjectival, *de* usually stands alone before the name of a country, province, or state.

Louis XIV est un célèbre roi de France.
Vous aimez cette histoire de Provence?

When the name is modified by an article and/or an adjective, *de* must combine with the article.

Les villes de la vieille Allemagne sont pittoresques.
L'histoire du Nouveau-Mexique est très intéressante.

POINTS OF THE COMPASS

These names are all masculine in French. They may also be combined, as in English. Notice that the *st* at the end of *l'est* and *l'ouest* is pronounced. The *r* of *nord* and the *d* of *sud* are also sounded.

le nord, le sud, l'est, l'ouest
le nord-est, le sud-ouest

Prepositions combine with the article in the usual way.

Chartres se trouve au sud-ouest de Paris.
Reims est à l'est de Rouen.
Nice est dans le sud de la France.

CONDITIONAL TENSE, INVERSION

DIRECTIONS: Complete each of the following examples by writing the correct form of the conditional tense on the numbered lines to the right.

1. *Elles* _____. (*donner*)

2. *Je* _____. (*finir*)

3. *Nous* _____. (*vendre*)

4. *Il* _____. (*faire*)

5. *Nous* _____. (*s'asseoir*)

6. *Je* _____. (*vouloir*)

7. *Elle* _____. (*devoir*)

8. *Vous* _____. (*aller*)

9. *Ils* _____. (*savoir*)

10. *Tu* _____. (*être*)

For each of the following sentences, write T (True) on the line at the right if it is correct and write F (False) if it is incorrect.

11. *S'il arriverait maintenant, il les verrait.*

12. *Elles étaient sûres qu'elles pourraient le voir bientôt.*

13. *Nous voudrions le faire sans votre aide.*

14. *Elle a dit qu'elle vendrait demain.*

15. *Souvent elle irait voir sa tante.*

16. *Le médecin a dit qu'elle mourait.*

17. *Même si je le faisais, il ne serait pas content.*

18. *Il devienne professeur, sans doute.*

19. *Si tout allait bien, il serait là.*

1 _____

2 _____

3 _____

4 _____

5 _____

6 _____

7 _____

8 _____

9 _____

10 _____

11 _____

12 _____

13 _____

14 _____

15 _____

16 _____

17 _____

18 _____

19 _____

BASIC FACTS

THE CONDITIONAL TENSE

The regular conditional tense is formed by adding the endings of the imperfect tense to the infinitive.

INFIN.	CONDITIONAL
donner	je donner**ais**
	tu donner**ais**
	il (elle) donner**ait**
	nous donner**ions**
	vous donner**iez**
	ils (elles) donner**aient**
finir	je finir**ais**, etc.
vendre	je vendr**ais**, etc.

Observe that 3rd conjugation verbs drop the final -*e* of the infinitive before adding the conditional endings. Verbs of the 4th conjugation, as always, are irregular. Any verb that has an irregular stem in the future tense has the same irregularity in the conditional.

INFIN.	FUTURE	COND.
aller	irai	irais
avoir	aurai	aurais
venir	viendrai	viendrais
voir	verrai	verrais

All compound verbs follow the same pattern.

devenir	deviendrai	deviendrais
retenir	retiendrai	retiendrais
renvoyer	renverrai	renverrais
revoir	reverrai	reverrais

As its name implies, the French conditional tense presents an event or an action that might happen. The implication is often that the event or action depends upon an "if" clause, whether such a clause is expressed or not.

S'il venait, je lui parlerais.
Je vous ai dit que je le ferais.

Notice that *si* (meaning "if") must be immediately followed by an imperfect tense when the verb in the other part of the sentence is in the conditional.

(*Continued on page 60*)

ADDITIONAL INFORMATION

OTHER USES OF THE CONDITIONAL TENSE

The conditional tense may be used in French, as in English, to make a sentence more formal or polite.

Voudriez-vous venir avec nous?
Pourrait-il le faire maintenant?
J'aimerais voir ce film.
Elle préférerait y aller ce soir.

Si (meaning "whether") requires the conditional tense.

Je ne savais pas s'ils viendraient.
Il m'a demandé s'il ferait beau en Espagne.
Nous n'étions pas sûrs si elle aurait assez de temps.
Vous demandiez-vous si je le verrais?

Remember that *si* (meaning "if") needs the imperfect or the present tense. *Quand même* (meaning "even if") takes the conditional tense in French and is followed by another conditional.

Quand même tu viendrais, je ne serais pas là.
Quand même nous le ferions, nous ne l'aimerions pas.
Quand même il y irait, il ne les trouverait pas.
Quand même il serait riche, il ne serait pas intelligent.

BUT: *Même si* (meaning "even if") follows the rules for *si*.

Au cas où (meaning "in case") requires the conditional tense and is followed by another conditional.

Au cas où elle perdrait son argent, elle aurait son billet.
Au cas où je le trouverais, je vous l'enverrais.
Au cas où il ne pourrait pas le faire, il me le dirait.
Au cas où son père mourrait, elle deviendrait riche.

SPELLING CHANGES

The same spelling changes occur in the conditional tense as in the future tense, for the same reasons.

INFIN.	PRESENT	FUTURE	CONDITIONAL
acheter	j'achète	j'achèterai	j'achèterais
appeler	j'appelle	j'appellerai	j'appellerais
céder	je cède	je cèderai	je cèderais
BUT: préférer	je préfère	je préférerai	je préférerais

INVERSION

When *aussi* is the first word in a sentence or clause, it means "therefore" or "so," and the pronoun subject and the verb must be inverted.

(*Continued on page 60*)

EXPLANATIONS

1. *Elles donneraient.* This is a regular form of the conditional; it is based on the infinitive plus the endings of the imperfect tense.

2. *Je finirais.* For the 2nd conjugation also, this is the correct form.

3. *Nous vendrions.* The 3rd conjugation drops the *e* of the infinitive.

4. *Il ferait. Faire* has an irregular conditional tense, like its future tense.

5. *Nous nous assiérions.* The pronoun object must agree with the subject. This conditional, like the future, is irregular.

6. *Je voudrais.* All verbs in the *-oir* group have irregular futures and conditionals.

7. *Elle devrait.* All French conditionals are patterned on the future tense. *Devoir* is irregular.

8. *Vous iriez. Aller* is irregular in its future and conditional tenses.

9. *Ils sauraient. Savoir,* like *avoir,* is irregular.

10. *Tu serais.* The verb *être* has irregular future and conditional tenses.

11. The sentence should read: *S'il arrivait maintenant, il les verrait. Si* (meaning "if") is never followed immediately by a future or conditional tense.

12. *Elles étaient sûres qu'elles pourraient le voir bientôt.* This sentence is correct because the imperfect describes a state of mind, and the conditional indicates what they *would be able* to do.

13. *Nous voudrions le faire sans votre aide. Voudrions* is a correct use of the conditional, meaning "would like."

14. The correct sentence would be: *Elle a dit qu'elle viendrait demain. Venir* has irregular future and conditional forms.

15. The sentence should read: *Souvent elle allait voir sa tante.* The imperfect is needed here for an action that is often repeated.

16. The correct version is: *Le médecin a dit qu'elle mourrait.* The future and conditional forms of *mourir* are irregular.

17. *Même si je le faisais, il ne serait pas content.* Like *si, même si* requires an imperfect, not a conditional.

18. The sentence should read: *Il deviendrait professeur, sans doute. Devenir* has the same irregularities as *venir.*

19. *Si tout allait bien, il serait là. Si* is correctly followed by the imperfect; the conditional is needed in the other part of the sentence.

Answers	
donneraient	1
finirais	2
vendrions	3
ferait	4
nous assiérions	5
voudrais	6
devrait	7
iriez	8
sauraient	9
serais	10
F	11
T	12
T	13
F	14
F	15
F	16
T	17
F	18
T	19

S'il le lisait, je serais content.
L'enverriez-vous si vous l'aviez?
Si j'étais vous, je n'y irais pas.
Il me le dirait si je le voulais.

Si (meaning "if") must never immediately precede the conditional or the future tense. Remember that in English the word "would" used in the imperfect sense means a repeated action; in French this construction requires the imperfect tense.

> *Tous les soirs il étudiait.*
> Every evening he would study.
> *Quand il était là, il le faisait.*
> When he was there, he would do it.
> *Elle le chantait pour lui.*
> She would sing it for him.

Beware also of the English word "should"; if it means "ought to" (in the sense of duty or obligation), the French equivalent requires the conditional tense of the verb *devoir*.

> *Je devrais leur écrire.*
> I should (ought to) write to them.
> *Vous devriez l'étudier.*
> You should (ought to) study it.
> BUT: *Je le ferais si j'étais vous.*
> I should (would) do it if I were you.

PROBABILITY

Like the future tense in French, the conditional may indicate probability; it can be translated as "no doubt," "probably," "do you suppose?" etc.

> *Où était-il? Il serait chez lui.*
> *Auraient-elles du travail à faire?*
> *Vous y iriez sans moi.*
> *Ils le feraient tout de même.*

Aussi la verrait-il le lendemain.
Therefore he would [probably] see her the following day.
Cette robe me va bien, aussi l'ai-je achetée.
This dress suits me well, so I bought it.

However, one may use *donc*, without inversion, instead of *aussi*.

> *Il la verrait donc le lendemain.*
> *Cette robe me va bien, donc je l'ai achetée.*

After *à peine* (meaning "scarcely" or "hardly") at the beginning of a sentence or clause, the following pronoun subject and verb must also be inverted:

> *A peine pouvions-nous les voir.*
> We could scarcely see them.
> *A peine le ferait-il sans moi.*
> He would hardly do it without me.
> BUT: *Nous pouvions à peine les voir.*
> *Il le ferait à peine sans moi.*

Peut-être (meaning "perhaps" or "maybe"), when it starts a sentence or clause, requires inversion in the same way.

> *Peut-être l'enverra-t-elle demain.*
> Perhaps she will send it tomorrow.
> *Peut-être le comprendriez-vous si vous le connaissiez.*
> Perhaps you would understand him if you knew him.
> BUT: *Elle l'enverra peut-être demain.*
> *Vous le comprendriez peut-être si vous le connaissiez.*

After spoken words the verb and its subject are again reversed.

> *« Bonjour », m'ont-ils dit.*
> "Good morning," they said to me.
> *« Bonjour », ai-je répondu.*
> "Good morning," I replied.
> BUT: *Ils m'ont dit bonjour.*
> *J'ai répondu bonjour.*

Sometimes there is inversion in French when the subject of each of the two verbs is a noun.

> *L'aventure qu'a racontée mon ami est incroyable.*
> The adventure my friend told about is unbelievable.
> *Le roman que décrit sa mère est intéressant.*
> The novel his mother describes is interesting.
> BUT: *L'aventure qu'il a racontée est incroyable.*
> *Le roman qu'elle décrit est intéressant.*

16

PLUPERFECT, PAST CONDITIONAL, TIME, WEATHER

SELF-TEST

DIRECTIONS: Match each of the following sentences with a verb selected from the list below, and write your answers on the numbered lines to the right.

1. *Il l'aurait fini s'il _____ le temps.*

    seraient partis

2. *Vous vouliez être sûr qu'elles _____ cela?*

    serait allé

3. *Elle _____ sur ce train-là.*

    aurions vendu

4. *Je me demande si vous _____ cela.*

    serait arrivée

5. *Il était sûr que nous _____ à l'heure.*

    avait eu

6. *Nous ne savons pas s'il y _____ .*

    aurait pris

7. *J'étais certain qu'ils _____ plus tôt.*

    seriez partis

8. *Si c'était possible, elle les _____ .*

    serions venus

9. *Vous _____ si elle y était allée.*

    avaient dit

10. *Il croyait que nous _____ l'auto.*

    auriez fait

Complete each of the following sentences with the correct form of time or weather.

11. *_____ deux heures quand nous sommes arrivés.* (It was)

12. *_____ mauvais aujourd'hui, n'est-ce pas?* (It is)

13. *Elle viendra à _____ .* (7:30)

14. *Demain _____ beau.* (it will be)

15. *Nous vous avons attendu pendant _____ .* (half an hour)

16. *Il faisait _____ quand nous sommes partis.* (sunny)

17. *Ils arriveront à dix heures _____ .* (P.M.)

18. *Maintenant il fait _____ .* (cold)

19. *Je partirai à _____ .* (4:40)

20. *Vous allez quitter la maison à _____ ?* (6:15)

1	_____
2	_____
3	_____
4	_____
5	_____
6	_____
7	_____
8	_____
9	_____
10	_____
11	_____
12	_____
13	_____
14	_____
15	_____
16	_____
17	_____
18	_____
19	_____
20	_____

BASIC FACTS

THE PLUPERFECT TENSE

The pluperfect is formed by the imperfect of the verb *avoir* or *être* plus the past participle of the main verb. The meanings are the same as in English.

INFIN.	PLUPERFECT
donner	j'avais donné, etc. (I had given)
finir	j'avais fini, etc. (I had finished)
vendre	j'avais vendu, etc. (I had sold)
voir	j'avais vu, etc. (I had seen)
avoir	j'avais eu, etc. (I had had)
être	j'avais été, etc. (I had been)

Verbs that are conjugated with *être* use its imperfect; they are also translated as "had" in English.

j'étais venu(e), etc. (I had come)
j'étais parti(e), etc. (I had left)

THE PAST CONDITIONAL TENSE

This tense is formed by the conditional tense of the verb *avoir* or *être* plus the past participle of the main verb.

INFIN.	PAST CONDITIONAL
donner	j'aurais donné, etc. (I would have given)
finir	j'aurais fini, etc. (I would have finished)
vendre	j'aurais vendu, etc. (I would have sold)
voir	j'aurais vu, etc. (I would have seen)
avoir	j'aurais eu, etc. (I would have had)
être	j'aurais été, etc. (I would have been)

The past conditional uses the condi-

(Continued on page 64)

ADDITIONAL INFORMATION

THE PLUPERFECT TENSE

The pluperfect tense specifies an action that had already taken place before the statement was made.

Nous avions fini notre devoir avant de nous coucher.
We had finished our work before going to bed.
Il était déjà parti quand nous sommes arrivés.
He had already left when we arrived.

Like the imperfect tense, the pluperfect directly follows *si* (meaning "if").

Si elle l'avait fait, nous le saurions.
If she had done it, we would know [it].
Seriez-vous content si je leur avais écrit?
Would you be pleased if I had written to them?

The pluperfect may also combine with a past conditional tense.

Ils l'auraient dit s'ils l'avaient trouvé.
They would have said [so] if they had found it.

THE PAST CONDITIONAL TENSE

The past conditional tense in French is used in much the same way as the conditional and may be combined with other tenses.

Je l'aurais fait si j'avais pu.
I would have done it if I could.
Si j'étais vous, je ne le ferais pas.
If I were you, I would not do it.

Like the conditional, the past conditional follows *si* (meaning "whether").

Nous ne savons pas si vous l'auriez fini.
We don't know whether you would have finished it.

TIME

Time of day requires the verb *être* and the noun *heure;* the verb *être* is always impersonal and singular.

Il est une heure.	It is 1:00.
Il était sept heures.	It was 7:00.

Since the hour is the most important element, the French take the nearest hour and add the minutes.

Il est six heures vingt.	It is 6:20.
Il était une heure vingt-neuf.	It was 1:29.

Fifteen and thirty minutes past the hour are usually expressed by *quart* and *demie,* preceded by *et.*

(Continued on page 64)

EXPLANATIONS

1. *Il l'aurait fini s'il* ***avait eu*** *le temps.* The pluperfect, like the imperfect, is used directly after *si* (if).

2. *Vous vouliez être sûr qu'elles* ***avaient dit*** *cela?* The pluperfect means simply "had said."

3. *Elle* ***serait arrivée*** *sur ce train-là.* The past conditional, like the conditional, indicates probability.

4. *Je me demande si vous* ***auriez fait*** *cela.* Like the conditional, the past conditional follows *si* (whether).

5. *Il était sûr que nous* ***serions venus*** *à l'heure.* The past conditional means simply "would have come."

6. *Nous ne savons pas s'il y* ***serait allé.*** The past conditional again follows *si* (whether).

7. *J'étais certain qu'ils* ***seraient partis*** *plus tôt.* Here the meaning is "would have left."

8. *Si c'était possible, elles les* ***aurait pris.*** Following an "if" clause, the past conditional is correct.

9. *Vous* ***seriez partis*** *si elle y était allée.* The past conditional correctly accompanies a pluperfect in an "if" clause.

10. *Il croyait que nous* ***aurions vendu*** *l'auto.* The past conditional is translated as "would have sold."

11. ***Il était*** *deux heures quand nous sommes arrivés.* Time in French requires the verb *être;* the imperfect tense indicates past time.

12. ***Il fait*** *mauvais aujourd'hui, n'est-ce pas?* Weather in French requires the verb *faire.*

13. *Elle viendra à* ***sept heures et demie.*** In French "half" rather than "thirty" is habitually used for the half hour; *demie* is feminine, agreeing with *heure.*

14. *Demain il fera beau.* Any tense of *faire* may indicate a weather condition.

15. *Nous avons attendu pendant* ***une demi-heure.*** When *demi* forms part of the noun, it remains invariable.

16. *Il faissait* ***du soleil*** *quand nous sommes partis.* When the weather element is visible, a noun is used with *faire.*

17. *Ils arriveront à dix heures* ***du soir.*** The term *du soir* is translated as "P.M." after 6 P.M.

18. *Maintenant il fait* ***froid.*** The adjective *froid* correctly denotes a weather condition.

19. *Je partirai à* ***cinq heures moins vingt.*** In French, the nearest hour is given and then the addition or subtraction of minutes.

20. *Vous allez quitter la maison à* ***six heures et quart.*** In French "quarter" is preferred to the number "fifteen" for the quarter hour.

Answers	
avait eu	1
avaient dit	2
serait arrivée	3
auriez fait	4
serions venus	5
serait allé	6
seraient partis	7
aurait pris	8
seriez partis	9
aurions vendu	10
Il était	11
Il fait	12
sept heures et demie	13
il fera	14
une demi-heure	15
du soleil	16
du soir	17
froid	18
cinq heures moins vingt	19
six heures et quart	20

tional of *être* for those verbs conjugated with it.

> *je serais venu(e)*, etc.
> (I would have come)
> *je serais parti(e)*, etc.
> (I would have left)

Remember that when the English word "should" means "ought to," it takes the verb *devoir* in French.

TIME (*L'Heure*)

French uses the verb *être* for the time of day, usually in the present or the imperfect tense.

> *Il est neuf heures.*
> It is 9:00.
> *Il était cinq heures.*
> It was 5:00.

The future and conditional tenses indicate probability.

> *Il sera trois heures à Paris.*
> It is probably 3:00 in Paris.
> *Il serait une heure quand il est arrivé.*
> It was probably 1:00 when he arrived.

Other tenses are not used for the time of day, and there is no term for "o'clock."

WEATHER (*Le Temps*)

Weather in French requires the verb *faire* in the 3rd person singular; the word *temps* is usually omitted.

> *Il fait beau aujourd'hui*
> It is fine today.
> *Il faisait mauvais hier.*
> It was bad weather yesterday.
> *Il fera chaud demain.*
> It will be hot tomorrow.
> *Il a fait froid ce matin.*
> It was cold this morning.

> *Il est trois heures et quart.*   It is 3:15.
> *Il était onze heures et demie.*   It was 11:30.

After the half hour, the next hour is the nearest, so the minutes or the quarter are substracted, preceded by *moins*.

> *Il est dix heures moins vingt-cinq.*   It is 9:35.
> *Il était sept heures moins dix.*   It was 6:50.
> *Il est neuf heures moins [le] quart.*   It is 8:45.

French translates "A.M." by the expression *du matin* and "P.M." by *de l'après midi*. Time after 6 P.M. requires *du soir*. The preposition *à* means "at."

> *Nous partirons à sept heures du matin.*
> We shall leave at 7 A.M.
> *Il est arrivé à trois heures de l'après-midi.*
> He arrived at 3 P.M.
> *Mon ami quittera Paris à huit heures du soir.*
> My friend will leave Paris at 8 P.M.

Midi replaces 12 noon, and *minuit* means 12 midnight.

> *Quelle heure est-il? [Il est] midi.*
> What time is it? [It is] noon.
> *A minuit ce sera le Nouvel An.*
> At midnight it will be the New Year.

For trains, planes, and most other public means of transportation, the 24-hour clock and the 60-minute hour replace the usual times.

> *Mon avion arrivera à six heures trente-cinq.*
> My plane will arrive at 6:35 A.M.
> *Le train part à vingt-trois heures.*
> The train leaves at 11 P.M.
> *Nous allons atterrir à dix-sept heures quarante-cinq.*
> We are going to land at 5:45 P.M.

WEATHER

Although in general the verb *faire* is used with an adjective to indicate a weather condition, when the condition is visible (sun, fog, mist), a noun replaces the adjective and is preceded by the partitive.

> *Il fait beau (mauvais, chaud, froid, frais, frisquet, bon).*
> It is fine (nasty, hot, cold, cool, chilly, nice).
> *Hier il faisait du soleil (du brouillard, de la brume).*
> Yesterday it was sunny (foggy, misty).

A definite weather action requires a verb instead of a noun or adjective.

pleuvoir	to rain	*neiger*	to snow
geler	to freeze	*grêler*	to hail
Aujourd'hui il pleut.	Today it's raining.		
Ce matin il a neigé.	This morning it snowed.		
Maintenant il gèle.	Now it's freezing.		
Demain il va grêler.	Tomorrow it's going to hail.		

17 FUTURE PERFECT, DISJUNCTIVE PRONOUNS; *SAVOIR, CONNAÎTRE*

DIRECTIONS: For each of the following sentences, write T (True) on the line at the right if it is correct and write F (False) if it is incorrect.

1. *Elle aura déjà finir avant midi.*

2. *Je l'aurai vu avant d'écrire la lettre.*

3. *Vous serez tous arrivés avant notre départ.*

4. *Ils seront été négligés par leurs parents.*

5. *Aussitôt que nous nous y serons installés, elle vous le dira.*

6. *Je sais votre père et votre mère.*

7. *Connaissez-vous la date de la Révolution française?*

8. *Il connaît bien Paris.*

9. *Elle sait l'importance de ce livre.*

10. *Ils me connaissent.*

Choose the appropriate form of the disjunctive personal pronoun, and write your answers (a, b, or c) on the lines to the right.

11. *Vous et _____?*
    a *me*   b *je*   c *moi*

12. *Elle va en France; _____, il reste à la maison.*
    a *il*   b *lui*   c *le*

13. *Les enfants, _____, vont à la plage.*
    a *ils*   b *eux*   c *les*

14. *Je viendrai avec _____, Jeanne et Marie.*
    a *elles*   b *eux*   c *ils*

15. *Quant à _____, tu ne seras pas là.*
    a *toi*   b *te*   c *tu*

16. *Qui est là? Notre amie. C'est _____!*
    a *lui*   b *la*   c *elle*

17. *Je les ai vus. Qui? _____!*
    a *Les*   b *Eux*   c *Elles*

1	_____
2	_____
3	_____
4	_____
5	_____
6	_____
7	_____
8	_____
9	_____
10	_____
11	_____
12	_____
13	_____
14	_____
15	_____
16	_____
17	_____

BASIC FACTS

THE FUTURE PERFECT TENSE

j'aurai	donné	(I will have
tu auras	donné	given, etc.)
il (elle) aura	donné
nous aurons	donné
vous aurez	donné
ils (elles) auront	donné

je serai	venu(e)	(I will have
tu seras	venu(e)	come, etc.)
il (elle) sera	venu(e)
nous serons	venu(e)s
vous serez	venu(s), venue(s)
ils (elles) seront	venu(e)s

The future perfect tense is formed by taking the future of *avoir* or *être* and adding the past participle of the active verb. Like other tenses, the future perfect uses *être* for those verbs conjugated with it, and the past participle agrees with the subject in the usual way.

Elle sera sortie.
She will have gone out.
Ils seront arrivés.
They will have arrived.

Reflexive verbs, as always, are conjugated with *être,* and the past participle agrees with the preceding direct object.

Je me serai lavé(e).
I will have washed [myself].
Nous nous serons arrêté(e)s.
We will have stopped.
Elles se seront habillées.
They will have dressed.
Il se sera réveillé.
He will have awakened.

Savoir

The verb *savoir* means to know a fact or a piece of information.

Savez-vous qu'il est arrivé?
Do you know [that] he has arrived?
Je le sais.
I know [it].

(Continued on page 68)

ADDITIONAL INFORMATION

THE FUTURE PERFECT TENSE

This tense is used mainly for an action in the future that will precede another future action. The second action often follows a preposition or a prepositional phrase. The meaning is literal.

Nous l'aurons fini avant ce soir.
We will have finished it before this evening.

If a verb is conjugated with *être,* the future perfect must also use *être* instead of *avoir.* In English it still means "to have."

Ils seront partis avant de vous voir.
They will have left before seeing you.

The future perfect tense, unlike the simple future tense, does not occur twice in the same sentence. The other verb generally denotes a straightforward future action.

Aussitôt que nous l'aurons fait, nous vous le donnerons.
As soon as we have (will have) done it, we'll give it to you.
Dès qu'elle sera arrivée, je viendrai ici.
As soon as she has (will have) arrived, I'll come here.

Like the simple future tense, the future perfect may indicate probability. Remember that the past participle must follow the rules of agreement.

Ils vous auront envoyé les lettres.
They have probably (will have) sent you the letters.
Les livres? Jean les aura rendus.
The books? John has probably (will have) returned them.

Savoir

Like the verb *avoir, savoir* has a contracted past participle and irregular future and conditional tenses.

INFIN.	PAST PART.	FUTURE	CONDIT.
avoir	eu	aurai	aurais
savoir	su	saurai	saurais

Savoir ordinarily means to know a fact or an idea; it can also be translated as "to know how to," and thus in this sense may replace the verb *pouvoir.*

Savez-vous nager?   Can you swim?

Savoir is also one of the few verbs that may omit the *pas* in a negative sentence and one *ni* in a "neither . . . nor" phrase.

(Continued on page 68)

EXPLANATIONS

1. The sentence should read: *Elle **aura** déjà **fini** avant midi.* Only a past participle may follow the verbs *avoir* and *être*.

2. *Je l'**aurai vu** avant d'écrire la lettre.* The future perfect correctly indicates an action that will precede another future action.

3. *Vous **serez** tous **arrivés** avant notre départ.* The future perfect is correctly used with *être*.

4. The sentence should read: *Ils **auront été** négligés par leurs parents.* The verb *être* is conjugated with *avoir*.

5. *Aussitôt que nous nous y **serons installés**, elle vous le dira.* The future perfect is correct for an action preceding another future action.

6. The correct sentence would be: *Je **connais** votre père et votre mère.* The verb *connaître* must be used for knowledge of a person.

7. The sentence should read: ***Savez**-vous la date de la Révolution française?* Knowledge of a fact calls for the verb *savoir*.

8. *Il **connaît** bien Paris.* Knowledge of a place, as well as a person, requires the verb *connaître*.

9. *Elle **sait** l'importance de ce livre.* Like Question 7, knowledge of a fact needs *savoir*.

10. *Ils me **connaissent**. Connaître* is correct for knowledge of a person.

11. *Vous et **moi?*** A pronoun standing alone must use its disjunctive or strong form.

12. *Elle va en France; **lui**, il reste à la maison.* Here the disjunctive pronoun form expresses comparison.

13. *Les enfants, **eux**, vont à la plage.* In this case the disjunctive pronoun is used for emphasis.

14. *Je viendrai avec **elles**, Jeanne et Marie.* Since both names are feminine, they require the plural pronoun *elles*.

15. *Quant à **toi**, tu ne seras pas là. Tu* becomes *toi* when it stands alone without a verb.

16. *Qui est là? Notre amie. C'est **elle!*** Since *amie* is feminine singular, it takes the pronoun *elle*.

17. *Je les ai vus. Qui? **Eux!** Les* in this case is masculine plural, and its disjunctive form is *eux*.

Answers

F	1
T	2
T	3
F	4
T	5
F	6
F	7
T	8
T	9
T	10
c	11
b	12
b	13
a	14
a	15
c	16
b	17

Est-elle ici?
Is she here?
Je ne sais pas.
I don't know.

Connaître

The verb *connaître* indicates knowledge of a person or a place.

Henri? Je ne le connais pas.
Henry? I don't know him.
Nous connaissons votre ville.
We know your town (city).

Disjunctive Personal Pronouns

moi	I, me
toi	you (fam. sing.)
lui	he, him, it (m.)
elle	she, her, it (f.)
nous	we, us
vous	you (sing. or plur.)
eux	they, them (m.)
elles	they, them (f.)

As the name implies, the disjunctive pronoun stands alone in the sentence, rather than as the subject of a verb.

Il est intelligent. Lui?
He is intelligent. He [is]?
Qui l'a fait? Moi.
Who did it? I [did].

The reflexive disjunctive pronoun is *soi*, as in *Chacun pour soi!* (Everyone for himself!) All these pronouns may also combine with *-même* (self).

Il l'a fait lui-même.
He did it himself.

Je ne sais si je devrais le faire.
I don't know if (whether) I ought to do it.
Il ne sait ni ne veut le dire.
He doesn't know how to nor does he want to say it.

In the compound tense *savoir* has a special meaning. *J'ai su* suggests, for example, "I found out" or "I learned."

Hier nous avons su qu'il est français.
Yesterday we found out [that] he is French.

Connaître

The verb *connaître* has a contracted past participle, *connu*, but its future and conditional tenses are regular—*connaîtrai, connaîtrais*. Ordinarily used for knowledge of a person or a place, *connaître* is also found in such expressions as *connaître de vue, connaître de nom*.

Vos parents? Je les connais de vue.
Your parents? I know them by sight.
Il connaît de nom notre professeur.
He knows our professor by name.

In the compound past tense *connaître* also has a special sense. *J'ai connu* means "I got to know" or "I met."

Hier elle a connu mes amis.
Yesterday she met my friends.
Ce matin vous avez connu mon frère?
Did you get to know my brother this morning?

Disjunctive Personal Pronouns

Disjunctive personal pronouns, required when the pronoun is not the direct subject of a verb, also form part of certain constructions.

After a preposition:

Elle arrivera avant moi ou après lui.
She will arrive before me or after him.

After *c'est* or *ce sont*:

C'est toi? Non, ce sont eux.
Is it you? No, it is they.

For emphasis:

Moi, je vais à Paris, mais lui, il va à Nice.
I am going to Paris, but **he** is going to Nice.

In a comparison:

Elle est plus intelligente que lui.
She is more intelligent than he [is].

Notice that the verb following a disjunctive pronoun must agree with that pronoun.

C'est nous qui l'avons fait.
We are the ones who did it.
Ce sont eux qui l'ont dit.
It's they who said it.

18 DEVOIR, FALLOIR, dans, en

DIRECTIONS: Select the appropriate forms of the verb *devoir* listed below for each of the following sentences, and write your answers on the lines to the right.

1. *Vous me _____ cinq francs.*   devaient

2. *Il _____ arriver à trois heures, mais il n'est pas venu.*   devrai

3. *Je _____ absolument y aller tout de suite.*   avez dû

4. *Elle _____ écrire plus souvent à sa mère.*   auriez dû

5. *Vous _____ les voir la semaine dernière.*   devraient

6. *Ils _____ le finir pour aujourd'hui.*   ont dû

7. *Vour _____ me le dire plus tôt.*   dois

8. *Voilà leurs livres! Ils _____ les oublier.*   devrait

9. *Je _____ le faire demain.*   devait

10. *Les grandes personnes _____ être plus intelligentes que les enfants.*   devez

Complete each of the following sentences by writing the appropriate positive or negative expression (*il faut, il ne faut pas, il est nécessaire, il n'est pas nécessaire*) on the numbered lines to the right.

11. *Il _____ toujours dire la vérité.* (positive)

12. *Il _____ d'aller à la gare.* (negative)

13. *Attention! Il _____ tomber.* (negative)

14. *Attendez! Il _____ passer par là.* (positive)

15. *Il _____ d'y arriver avant ce soir.* (positive)

16. *Mais j'insiste! Il _____ y manger.* (negative)

17. *Tous les jours, il _____ d'y faire attention.* (positive)

18. *Non! Il _____ le dire!* (negative)

19. *Calmez-vous! Il _____ de vous exciter.* (negative)

20. *Malheureusement, il _____ d'y aller.* (positive)

1 _____
2 _____
3 _____
4 _____
5 _____
6 _____
7 _____
8 _____
9 _____
10 _____
11 _____
12 _____
13 _____
14 _____
15 _____
16 _____
17 _____
18 _____
19 _____
20 _____

BASIC FACTS

Devoir

This verb has various meanings in English such as "to be obliged to," "to have to," "to be supposed to," and "to owe." It also means "must," "should," and "ought to." It needs no preposition before a following infinitive.

INFIN.	devoir
PRES. PART.	devant
PAST PART.	dû (due)
PRES. INDIC.	dois, dois, doit, devons, devez, doivent
IMPERF.	devais, etc.
FUTURE	devrai, etc.
CONDIT.	devrais, etc.
COMP. PAST	j'ai dû, etc.
PLUPERFECT	j'avais dû, etc.
FUT. PERF.	j'aurai dû, etc.
PAST CONDIT.	j'aurais dû, etc.

Falloir

This verb is always impersonal and therefore appears only in the 3rd person with the pronoun *il;* it implies a strong sense of necessity. *Falloir* may be used in any tense and does not require a preposition before a following infinitive. In the negative it means "must not."

Il faut partir tout de suite.
It's necessary to leave at once.
(We [you, they, she, I, etc.] must leave at once.)
Il faut admettre ses défauts.
It is necessary to admit one's faults.
(One must admit one's faults.)
Il ne faut pas y entrer.
One (we, you, etc.) must not go in there.

Il Est Nécessaire

This adjectival phrase expresses less urgent necessity. It needs *de* before a following infinitive.

Il est nécessaire d'étudier.
It is necessary to study.

(Continued on page 72)

ADDITIONAL INFORMATION

Devoir

Devoir refers to a personal and usually moral obligation, rather than to a necessity imposed by outside forces. The verb may be used in any tense and in any person since it is complete. The difficulty lies in translating it into English because there are so many paraphrases.

PRES.   *Nous devons le faire bientôt.*
We must (have to, are [supposed] to) do it soon.
Je vous dois dix dollars.
I owe you ten dollars.

Notice that the English words "is to" or "are to" indicate obligation and therefore must be translated by the present tense of *devoir*. Notice also the difference between the following examples:

Vous devez faire du travail.   You have to do some work.
Vous avez du travail à faire.   You have some work to do.

IMPERF.   *Vous deviez arriver hier soir.*
You were [supposed] to arrive last night.

Like the present tense, the expressions "was to" and "were to" imply obligation; they require the imperfect of *devoir*.

FUTURE   *Elle devra le lui dire demain.*
She will have to tell it (that) to him tomorrow.
CONDIT.   *Nous devrions les attendre ici.*
We should (ought to) wait for them here.

Notice particularly the wording "should" or "ought to," which must not be confused with the normal conditional "would" of other verbs.

COMP. PAST   *Où sont mes gants? J'ai dû les laisser chez Marie.*
Where are my gloves? I must have left them at Mary's.

Notice that the English verbal meaning is simply reversed in French. The past participle *dû* has a circumflex accent to distinguish it from the partitive article *du*. The feminine past participle does not have an accent because there is no similar form.

PLUP.   *Il avait dû le mettre dans un tiroir.*
He had had to put it into a drawer.
FUT. PERF.   *Avant d'y arriver, vous aurez dû voyager longtemps.*
Before arriving there, you will have had to travel a long time.
PAST COND.   *Ils auraient dû me l'envoyer hier.*
They should (ought to) have sent it to me yesterday.

(Continued on page 72)

EXPLANATIONS

1. *Vous me **devez** cinq francs. Devoir* may mean "to owe," especially in the present tense.

2. *Il **devait** arriver à trois heures, mais il n'est pas venu.* The imperfect means "was supposed to."

3. *Je **dois** absolument y aller tout de suite.* Urgency, in the sense of "must," requires the present tense.

4. *Elle **devrait** écrire plus souvent à sa mère.* Obligation ("should" or "ought to") calls for the conditional tense.

5. *Vous **avez dû** les voir la semaine dernière.* The compound past tense is translated as "must have."

6. *Ils **devaient** le finir pour aujourd'hui.* The imperfect again means "were supposed to."

7. *Vous **auriez dû** me le dire plus tôt.* "Should have" requires the past conditional tense.

8. *Voilà leurs livres! Ils **ont dû** les oublier.* "Must have," like Question 5, needs the compound past tense.

9. *Je **devrai** le faire demain.* The future tense expresses a future action.

10. *Les grandes personnes **devraient** être plus intelligentes que les enfants.* The conditional translates as "should" or "ought to."

11. *Il **faut** toujours dire la vérité.* The verb *falloir* correctly indicates a strong necessity.

12. *Il **n'est pas nécessaire** d'aller à la gare.* The impersonal phrase with an adjective must precede the preposition *de*.

13. *Attention! Il **ne faut pas** tomber.* The negative of *falloir* is always very strong and means "must not."

14. *Attendez! Il **faut** passer par là.* The verb *falloir* is not followed by a preposition.

15. *Il **est nécessaire** d'y arriver avant ce soir.* The adjectival phrase again precedes the preposition *de*.

16. *Mais j'insiste! Il **ne faut pas** y manger.* The sense of "must not" requires the negative of *falloir*.

17. *Tous les jours, il **est nécessaire** d'y faire attention.* Like Questions 12 and 15, the adjectival phrase is followed by *de*.

18. *Non! Il **ne faut pas** le dire.* The strong negative needs *falloir*.

19. *Calmez-vous! Il **n'est pas nécessaire** de vous exciter.* The milder negative is translated by the adjectival expression with *de*.

20. *Malheureusement, il **est nécessaire** d'y aller.* The preposition *de* requires the adjectival phrase.

Answers	
devez	1
devait	2
dois	3
devrait	4
avez dû	5
devaient	6
auriez dû	7
ont dû	8
devrai	9
devraient	10
faut	11
n'est pas nécessaire	12
ne faut pas	13
faut	14
est nécessaire	15
ne faut pas	16
est nécessaire	17
ne faut pas	18
n'est pas nécessaire	19
est nécessaire	20

In its negative form, this expression does not mean "must not," but can simply be taken literally.

> *Il n'est pas nécessaire d'y entrer.*
> It is not necessary to go in there.

dans

This preposition literally means "inside" a place of fairly limited space.

> *Il est dans sa chambre.*
> He is in his [bed]room.
> *Marie est dans l'hôtel.*
> Mary is in the hotel.
> *Il y a un musée dans la ville.*
> There is a museum in the town.
> *Les poissons vivent dans l'eau.*
> Fish live in the water.
> *On a confiance dans le monde.*
> One has confidence in the world.
> *Dans les provinces il n'y a rien.*
> In the provinces there is nothing.

en

En means "in" when the limits are less precise and more indefinite.

> *Je vais à la plage en été.*
> I go to the beach in summer.
> *En général, j'aime le cinéma.*
> In general, I like the movies.
> *Elle m'écrit en français.*
> She writes to me in French.
> *Ils sont en Alsace.*
> They are in Alsace.
> *Avez-vous été en France?*
> Have you been in France?
> *Il habite en Amérique.*
> He lives in America.
> *Le ballon va en haut.*
> The balloon is going up.

Besides accompanying words that refer to wider, less tangible limits, *en* follows *de* in phrases meaning "from . . . to," and for the end of a time period.

> *J'y vais de temps en temps.*
> I go there from time to time.
> *On peut y arriver en six heures.*
> One can arrive there in six hours.

Like the simple conditional, the past conditional is translated as "ought to" or "should" when in the past time.

Falloir

This verb, like *devoir*, indicates obligation, but of a stronger and more impersonal nature because of forces outside the individual such as time, regulations, etc. In French the verb must be used impersonally, but it can appear in any tense and may apply to any person. The past participle is *fallu*.

PRES.   *Il faut étudier les leçons maintenant.*
One (I, we, you, they, he, she) must study the lessons now.

IMPERF.   *Il fallait le faire tous les jours.*
It was necessary to do it every day.
(One [I, you, etc.] had to do it every day.)

FUTURE   *Il faudra aller les voir demain.*
It will be necessary to go and see them tomorrow.
(One [I, you, etc.] will have to go and see them tomorrow.)

CONDIT.   *Il faudrait stationner la voiture là-bas.*
It would be necessary to park the car over there.
(One [I, you, etc.] would have to park the car over there.)

Similarly: *Hier il a fallu étudier* (comp. past), etc.

dans

In addition to indicating fairly precise limits, *dans* is generally used in sentences with a definite article.

> *Dans le cas de mon ami, il n'était pas à blâmer.*
> In my friend's case, he was not to blame.

Dans also occurs in expressions specifying time limits.

> *Je le paierai dans dix jours.*   I'll pay it within ten days.

en

En is often used with a personal pronoun, a possessive or demonstrative adjective, a noun without an article, and the article *des*.

> *Vous avez confiance en lui (en ses amis)?*
> You have confidence in him (in his friends)?
> *En ce cas, je m'en vais.*
> In that case, I'm going [away].
> *La vie est plus facile en province.*
> Life is easier in the provinces.
> *En des circonstances pareilles, je comprends.*
> In such circumstances, I understand.

19

PRESENT SUBJUNCTIVE;
COMME, COMMENT, QUE

SELF-TEST

DIRECTIONS: For each of the following sentences, write T (True) on the line at the right if it is correct and write F (False) if it is incorrect.

1. *Il n'est pas sûr qu'elle viendra.*

2. *Voulez-vous que je le fasse?*

3. *Craint-il qu'elles viennent?*

4. *Nous sommes heureux qu'il vous connaît.*

5. *Elle ne croit pas que vous puissiez le faire.*

6. *Pensez-vous qu'ils y vont?*

7. *Il doute que vous le sachiez.*

8. *Essayez de le faire sans qu'elle le sait.*

9. *Pourvu que nous arrivons à temps, c'est bien.*

10. *Bien que je ne les connaisse pas, je ne les aime pas.*

Complete each of the following sentences by writing the appropriate word for "how," "as," or "like" (*comme, comment*) on the numbered lines to the right.

11. _____ *le fait-il?*

12. _____ *nous avons dit, elle est gentille.*

13. _____ *vous, ils aiment danser.*

14. *Je ne sais pas* _____ *nous l'avons fait.*

15. *Vous l'avez écrit* _____ *si vous le compreniez.*

16. *Il joue* _____ *un ange.*

17. *Elle va le faire.* _____?

18. *Vous pouvez faire* _____ *vous voudrez.*

19. _____ *ils sont intelligents!*

20. *Il est parti* _____ *s'il avait peur.*

BASIC FACTS

SUBJUNCTIVE MOOD, PRESENT TENSE

INFIN. donner
PRES. INDIC. **donn**ons
PRES. SUBJ. (que) je donne
       tu donnes
       il (elle) donne
       nous donnions
       vous donniez
       ils (elles) donnent

The present tense of the subjunctive is formed from the stem of the first person plural of the present indicative, plus the endings *-e, -es, -e, -ions, -iez, -ent*. All forms of the subjunctive are generally preceded by *que* to indicate that they are in a subordinate clause that depends upon a preceding main verb.

INFIN.	PRES. INDIC.	PRES. SUBJ.
finir	**finiss**ons	(que) je finisse
vendre	**vend**ons	(que) je vende

The subjunctive mood usually suggests a doubt, uncertainty, or possibility, depending upon the mood created by the preceding main verb's indicative tense. The subjects of the two verbs must not be the same.

Nous avons peur qu'elle le sache.
We are afraid [that] she may know it.
(We are afraid [that] she knows it.)
Il doute que vous le fassiez.
He doubts [that] you are doing it.
(He doubts [that] you will do it.)

Notice the ways in which these sentences may be translated into English. Even when an emotion is followed by a fact, the emotion requires the subjunctive in the following clause.

Ils sont tristes qu'elle vienne.
They are sad [that] she is coming.

A wish or command involving another person also needs the subjunctive for the dependent verb.

Elle veut qu'il le sache.
She wants him to know it.

(Continued on page 76)

ADDITIONAL INFORMATION

SUBJUNCTVE MOOD, PRESENT TENSE

The main irregular subjunctive forms in the present tense are as follows:

aller	aille, ailles, aille, allions, alliez, aillent
avoir	aie, aies, ait, ayons, ayez, aient
connaître	connaisse, connaisses, connaisse, etc.
dire	dise, dises, dise, disions, disiez, disent
écrire	écrive, écrives, écrive, écrivions, écriviez, etc.
être	sois, sois, soit, soyons, soyez, soient
faire	fasse, fasses, fasse, fassions, fassiez, fassent
pouvoir	puisse, puisses, puisse, puissions, puissiez, etc.
recevoir	reçoive, reçoives, reçoive, recevions, receviez, reçoivent
savoir	sache, saches, sache, sachions, sachiez, sachent
venir	vienne, viennes, vienne, venions, veniez, viennent
voir	voie, voies, voie, voyions, voyiez, voient
vouloir	veuille, veuilles, veuille, voulions, vouliez, veuillent

Notice the irregularities within the tenses of the verbs *aller, avoir, recevoir, venir,* and *vouloir,* also the spelling changes in *être* and *voir.* The verb *(s')asseoir* is also irregular: *asseye, asseyions,* or *assoye, assoyions,* etc.

The subjunctive always occurs in a dependent clause, following *que,* and never as the main verb. The only exception to this is in a phrase, with or without *que,* in which the main verb is not expressed.

Vive le Président! (Je veux que le Président vive longtemps!)
Long live the President! (I wish the President may live long!)
Qu'ils entrent! (Je veux qu'ils entrent!)
Let them enter! (I want them to enter!)
Qu'elle meure! (Je veux qu'elle meure!)
Let her die! (I want her to die!) (I wish that she might die.)

The impersonal verb *falloir* may also use *que* and a subjunctive if there is a change of subject.

Il faut y aller.   It is necessary to go there.
Il faut que vous y alliez. It is necessary that you go there.

Other impersonal expressions also need *que* and the subjunctive if the subject changes.

Il est nécessaire de le savoir.
It is necessary to know it.
Il est nécessaire qu'ils le sachent.
It is necessary that they [should] know it.

(Continued on page 76)

EXPLANATIONS

1. This sentence should read: *Il n'est pas sûr qu'elle **vienne.*** Since there is uncertainty, the following verb must be in the subjunctive mood.

2. *Voulez-vous que je le **fasse?*** Because the action depends upon someone else's wish, it will not necessarily be accomplished; therefore, the subjunctive is required.

3. *Craint-il qu'elles **viennent?*** The subjunctive is necessary after expressions of emotion.

4. The correct sentence would be: *Nous sommes heureux qu'il vous **connaisse.*** The subjunctive must follow a phrase of emotion even if the statement is a fact.

5. *Elle ne croit pas que vous **puissiez** le faire.* This is correct because her lack of belief creates a doubt.

6. This sentence should be: *Pensez-vous qu'ils y **aillent?*** Interrogative forms imply a doubt, requiring use of the subjunctive.

7. *Il doute que vous le **sachiez.*** The subjunctive is correct after expressions of doubt.

8. The correct sentence would be: *Essayez de le faire sans qu'elle le **sache.*** *Sans que* is one of several conjunctions that require the subjunctive.

9. This sentence should read: *Pourvu que nous **arrivions** à temps, c'est bien.* The subjunctive must follow the conjunction *pourvu que*.

10. *Bien que je ne les **connaisse** pas, je ne les aime pas. Bien que* also requires the subjunctive.

11. ***Comment** le fait-il?* "How?" (meaning "in what way?") requires *comment* in French.

12. ***Comme** nous avons dit, elle est gentille. Comme* means "as" or "like."

13. ***Comme** vous, ils aiment danser.* "Like" is correctly translated by *comme*.

14. *Je ne sais pas **comment** nous l'avons fait. Comment* expresses the word "how."

15. *Vous l'avez écrit **comme** si vous le compreniez.* "As" or "as if" needs the French word *comme*.

16. *Il joue **comme** un ange.* As in Question 13, *comme* means "like."

17. *Elle va le faire. **Comment?*** Like Question 11, this is a question, translated as "how?"

18. *Vous pouvez faire **comme** vous voudrez. Comme* means "as" in this sentence.

19. ***Comme** ils sont intelligents!* An exclamatory "how" is *comme* in French, not *comment*.

20. *Il est parti **comme** s'il avait peur.* As in Question 15, *comme* precedes *si*, meaning "as if."

Answers	
F	1
T	2
T	3
F	4
T	5
F	6
T	7
F	8
F	9
T	10
Comment	11
Comme	12
Comme	13
comment	14
comme	15
comme	16
Comment	17
comme	18
Comme	19
comme	20

An expression of certainty, when negative or interrogative, creates a doubt, thereby requiring the subjunctive in the subordinate (dependent) clause.

> *Croyez-vous qu'ils le veuillent?*
> Do you think [that] they want it?
> *Elle n'est pas sûre qu'il l'ait.*
> She is not sure [that] he has it.

Conjunctions Requiring the Subjunctive

à moins que	although
afin que, pour que	in order that
avant que	before
bien que, quoi que	although
de crainte que	for fear that
jusqu'à ce que	until
pourvu que	provided that
sans que	without

> *Partons, à moins qu'il soit trop tard.*
> Let's leave, unless it is too late.

Comme, Comment

Comme combines with a noun or pronoun to mean "like."

> *Il est bête, comme sa soeur.*
> He is stupid, like his sister.

When *comme* precedes a verb, it is translated as "as," sometimes followed by *si* (if).

> *Comme vous le savez, il est jeune.*
> As you know, he is young.
> *Je le dis comme si je le voulais.*
> I say it as if I wanted to.

In .an exclamation, *comme* means "how!" Notice the French word order.

> *Comme elle est belle!*
> How beautiful she is!

Comment retains the adverbial sense of "how?" or "in what way?" It may also occur in an exclamation meaning "what!"

> *Comment l'avez-vous fait?*
> How did you do it?
> *Comment! Ils sont morts?*
> What! They are dead?

> *Il est bon qu'elle le fasse.*
> It is good that she should do (does) it.

Do not confuse this use of the English word "should" with the meaning "ought to." The latter takes the verb *devoir*. Other impersonal phrases needing *que* and the subjunctive before a change of subject are:

il est juste	it is right
il est important	it is important
il est possible	it is possible

All these expressions indicate a possibility, not a fact. Notice that the interrogative or negative forms of expressions of fact must also be followed by the subjunctive when the subject changes.

> *Est-il vrai qu'elle vienne?*
> Is it true [that] she is coming?
> *Il n'est pas sûr (certain) qu'elle le sache.*
> It is not certain [that] she knows it.

ALSO: *Il est peu probable qu'elle le fasse.*
> It is unlikely [that] she is doing it.

BUT: *Il est probable qu'elle vient.*
> It is probable [that] she is coming.
> *Il est évident que vous le savez.*
> It is obvious [that] you know it.
> *Il est certain qu'ils le font.*
> It is certain [that] they are doing it.

Comme, Que

Que may replace *comme* (how) in an exclamatory statement. Notice the French word order.

> *Comme vous êtes intelligent! (Que vous êtes intelligent!)*
> How intelligent you are!
> *Qu'il est beau, votre fils! Comme il est beau!*
> How handsome your son is! How handsome he is!

Comme is generally followed by *si* to mean "as if," but an exception occurs when the preposition *pour* follows with an infinitive.

> *Elle a fait un geste comme pour dire « Je proteste.»*
> She made a gesture as if to say "I protest."

Another idiomatic use of *comme* occurs with *qui* and a conditional tense.

> *Il parle comme qui voudrait dire le contraire.*
> He speaks like [some]one who would like to say the contrary.

Comme may also mean "as a" when appearing alone in front of a noun.

> *Comme parent, il est excellent.*
> As a parent, he is excellent.
> *Je vous prends comme témoin.*
> I take you as a witness.

20 POSSESSIVE PRONOUNS; à, avec, de

DIRECTIONS: Select the appropriate possessive pronoun listed below for each of the following sentences, and write your answers on the lines to the right.

1. *Voilà mes livres. Où sont* _____? (yours)		*le mien*
2. *C'est son amie et* _____. (mine)		*la leur*
3. *Voici nos cartes. Et* _____? (his)		*le nôtre*
4. *Ce parapluie? C'est* _____. (mine)		*la mienne*
5. *Tu aimes ma maison? Et j'aime* _____. (yours)		*les vôtres*
6. *Voilà son portrait et* _____. (ours)		*les siennes*
7. *Sa maison est près de* _____. (theirs)		*les nôtres*
8. *Vous avez mon sac et* _____? (hers)		*les miens*
9. *Ses amis et* _____ *se connaissent.* (ours)		*la tienne*
10. *Ce sont les gants de Marie? Non, ce sont* _____. (mine)		*le sien*

For each of the following sentences, write T (True) on the line at the right if it is correct and write F (False) if it is incorrect.

11. *La terre est couverte de neige.*

12. *L'homme avec les cheveux blonds est Robert.*

13. *Il joue avec sincérité.*

14. *Le jardin est entouré avec des arbres.*

15. *L'enfant avec le visage sérieux est intelligent.*

16. *La dame à la robe blanche est ma soeur.*

17. *Ils parlent avec la joie.*

18. *J'y vais avec mes amis.*

19. *Le garçon des mains grosses est dans votre classe.*

20. *La petite fille aux yeux bleus est sa nièce.*

1 _____
2 _____
3 _____
4 _____
5 _____
6 _____
7 _____
8 _____
9 _____
10 _____
11 _____
12 _____
13 _____
14 _____
15 _____
16 _____
17 _____
18 _____
19 _____
20 _____

BASIC FACTS

POSSESSIVE PRONOUNS

SINGULAR

MASC.	FEM.	
le mien	la mienne	(mine)
le tien	la tienne	(yours, fam.)
le sien	la sienne	(his, hers, its)
le nôtre	la nôtre	(ours)
le vôtre	la vôtre	(yours)
le leur	la leur	(theirs)

PLURAL

les miens	les miennes
les tiens	les tiennes
les siens	les siennes
les nôtres	les nôtres
les vôtres	les vôtres
les leurs	les leurs

Notice that the words "ours," "yours," and "theirs" have no separate feminine forms and that only the article distinguishes the singular forms. The article must always be included. Remember that, as always in French, the adjective or pronoun must agree with the specific noun and *not* with the owner.

sa maison et la leur
his house and theirs
ton livre et le nôtre
your book and ours
leurs idées et les miennes
their ideas and mine
votre voiture et la sienne
your car and his (hers)
mes lettres et les siennes
my letters and hers (his)

Usually the context determines whether the meaning is "his" or "hers." If not, the sentence must be changed to make the sense clear.

votre voiture et la sienne
votre voiture et celle de Robert
mes lettres et les siennes
mes lettres et celles de Marie

(Continued on page 80)

ADDITIONAL INFORMATION

POSSESSIVE PRONOUNS

The definite article of these pronouns combines with the prepositions *à* and *de* in the usual way.

Il va en envoyer à son frère et au mien.
He is going to send some to his brother and [to] mine.
Je parle de mes parents et des vôtres.
I'm talking about my parents and [about] yours.
Que pensez-vous de mon livre et du sien?
What do you think of my book and [of] his?

To indicate possession, the preposition *à* plus the disjunctive pronoun often replaces the possessive pronoun.

Ces photos sont à lui.
These (those) photos are his (belong to him).
Est-ce que cette voiture est à eux?
Is this car theirs? (Does this car belong to them?)

But the possessive pronoun together with the verb *être* emphasizes ownership.

Cette chambre-ci est la sienne.
This [bed]room is **his** (not anyone else's).

à

Besides being required for a description, *à* may mean "in" ("according to").

Laissez-moi tranquille. Je le ferai à ma manière.
Leave me alone. I'll do it in my own way.
C'est un vrai savant, à sa façon.
He is a real scholar, in his own way.

avec, sans

Like *avec*, *sans* accompanies a pronoun, or a noun with an article.

Vous allez avec ou sans lui?
Are you going with or without him?
J'arriverai sans mes amis.
I'll arrive without my friends.
Nous viendrons sans l'auto.
We'll come without the car.

Sans and *avec* also combine with a noun in an adverbial phrase without an article.

Il travaille avec (sans) difficulté.
He works with (without) difficulty.
Ils le feront sans bruit.
They will do it without noise (noiselessly).

(Continued on page 80)

EXPLANATIONS

1. *Voilà mes livres. Où sont **les vôtres?*** This pronoun refers to plural books, and, like an adjective, must agree with it in number and gender.

2. *C'est son amie et **la mienne.** Amie* is feminine singular and thus requires a similar pronoun.

3. *Voilà nos cartes. Et **les siennes?*** This pronoun agrees with the feminine plural *cartes*.

4. *Ce parapluie? C'est **le mien.*** This masculine singular noun needs a pronoun that agrees.

5. *Tu aimes ma maison? Et j'aime **la tienne.*** The familiar subject *tu* must have the feminine singular familiar pronoun to agree with *maison*.

6. *Voilà son portrait et **le nôtre.** Portrait* is masculine singular, and so is *le nôtre*.

7. *Sa maison est près de **la leur.** La leur* agrees with *maison*.

8. *Vous avez mon sac et **le sien?** Le sien* must match the noun *sac* in gender and number.

9. *Ses amis et **les nôtres** se connaissent.* This noun is masculine plural, and so is the pronoun.

10. *Ce sont les gants de Marie? Non, ce sont **les miens.** Les miens* refers to the masculine plural *gants*.

11. *La terre est couverte **de** neige.* A description of an object usually requires *de* for "with."

12. This sentence should read: *L'homme **aux** cheveux blonds est Robert.* A physical description of a person needs *à* and the definite article to mean "with."

13. *Il joue **avec** sincérité. Avec* is usually translated as "with" when there is action.

14. The correct sentence would be: *Le jardin est entouré **d'**arbres.* Like Question 11, this sentence requires *de* for a description of an object.

15. The correct version would be: *L'enfant **au** visage sérieux est intelligent.* For a physical description of a person, *à* is used.

16. *La dame **à la** robe blanche est ma soeur. A la* is correct for this physical description of a person.

17. This sentence should read: *Ils parlent **avec** joie.* An action or manner should have *avec* before the noun.

18. *J'y vais **avec** mes amis. Avec* here literally means "together with."

19. The correct sentence would be: *Le garçon **aux** mains grosses est dans votre classe.* Physical description must have *à*.

20. *La petite fille **aux** yeux bleus est sa nièce.* The personal descriptive phrase "with blue eyes" requires *aux*.

Answers

les vôtres	1
la mienne	2
les siennes	3
le mien	4
la tienne	5
le nôtre	6
la leur	7
le sien	8
les nôtres	9
les miens	10
T	11
F	12
T	13
F	14
F	15
T	16
F	17
T	18
F	19
T	20

à, avec, de

Each of these prepositions may express the English word "with" in a different context.

à

This word plus the definite article is translated as "with" in the description of a person.

> *la jeune fille **aux** yeux tristes*
> the girl with the sad eyes
> *le père **au** visage bruni*
> the father with the tanned face
> *l'homme **au** veston sale*
> the man with the dirty jacket

The word *à* may also be used in describing an animal, plant, or even an object.

> *le chien **au** poil blanc*
> the dog with the white fur (hair)
> *ces roses **à la** belle couleur*
> these roses with the lovely color
> *le livre **à la** couverture noire*
> the book with the black cover

avec

This preposition means "with" in the literal sense of "together with."

> *Vous venez avec moi?*
> Are you coming with me?
> *Il y va avec le professeur.*
> He goes there with the teacher.

Avec also occurs in an adverbial phrase, before a noun without an article.

> *Il le fait avec soin.*
> He does it with care (carefully).
> *Elle parle avec emphase.*
> She speaks emphatically.

de

This preposition is translated as "with" or "by" in a description immediately preceding a second noun, generally without an article.

> *le tableau encadré de bois*
> the picture framed with (by) wood
> *le pot rempli d'eau*
> the jug filled with water

In addition, *sans* is used with an infinitive.

> *Elle est partie sans parler.*
> She left without speaking.
> *On ne peut pas réussir sans travailler.*
> One cannot succeed without working.

de

This preposition has other meanings besides "of" and "from." In a description it may be translated as "by," "with," or "of" when followed by a noun without an article.

> *La maison est entourée de champs.*
> The house is surrounded by fields.
> *La mer est remplie de poissons.*
> The sea is filled with fish.
> *C'est une table de bois.*
> It is a wooden table (a table of wood).

Other descriptive phrases also include *de* (meaning "by"), often following a past participle.

> *Où est Jean? Le voilà, suivi de son chien.*
> Where is John? There he is, followed by his dog.
> *Marie est aimée de tous ses camarades.*
> Mary is loved by all her companions.

De may also be translated as the preposition "in" or "with" in an adverbial construction.

> *De quelle façon l'ont-ils fait?*
> In what way did they do it?
> *Elle a répondu d'un geste fatigué.*
> She replied with a tired gesture.
> *Vous parlez d'un air gêné.*
> You speak with an embarrassed look.

Notice also the following example:

> *La façon (manière) dont il joue est agréable.*
> The way he plays is pleasant.
> (The way in which he plays is pleasant.)

21

PAST SUBJUNCTIVE;
PARTIR, QUITTER, LAISSER

DIRECTIONS: Choose the correct form of the verb, and write your answers (a, b, c, d, or e) on the lines to the right.

1. *Est-il nécessaire qu'elle* _____ *cela?*
   a *fut*   b *fit*   c *ait fait*
   d *fusse*   e *a fait*

2. *C'est bien, pourvu que vous y* _____ ____.
   a *allez*   b *soyez allés*
   c *êtes allés*   d *iriez*
   e *irez*

3. *Il est vrai que je les* _____.
   a *voie*   b *aie vus*   c *visse*
   d *ai vus*   e *a vu*

4. *Je crains qu'il* _____.
   a *soit venu*   b *est venu*

   c *vient*   d *vint*
   e *viendra*

5. *Elle est contente que vous l'* _____.
   a *avez reçu*   b *ayez reçu*
   c *aurez reçu*   d *reçussiez*
   e *recevez*

6. *Êtes-vous sûr qu'ils* _____ *l'auto?*
   a *vendirent*   b *vendront*
   c *aient vendu*   d *ont vendu*
   e *vendaient*

7. *Nous espérons que tu le lui* _____.
   a *donne*   b *donnez*
   c *donna*   d *aies donné*
   e *as donné*

Choose the correct verb, and write your answers (a, b, or c) on the lines to the right.

8. *Il doit* _____ *Paris demain.*
   a *partir*   b *quitter*   c *laisser*

9. *J'ai* _____ *mes livres chez vous.*
   a *laissé*   b *quitté*   c *parti*

10. *Vous voulez* _____?
    a *quitter*   b *laisser*   c *partir*

11. *Elle va* _____ *de New York.*
    a *laisser*   b *partir*   c *quitter*

12. *Nous avons* _____ *nos amis ce matin.*
    a *parti*   b *laissé*   c *quitté*

1	
2	
3	
4	
5	
6	
7	
8	
9	
10	
11	
12	

BASIC FACTS

PAST TENSE, SUBJUNCTIVE MOOD

The past, or compound, tense of the subjunctive mood is formed in the same way as the compound past tense of the indicative mood, but using the present subjunctive of *avoir* or *être* plus the past participle of the verb of action.

avoir	*être*
aie	sois
aies	sois
ait	soit
ayons	soyons
ayez	soyez
aient	soient

The past subjunctive is used whenever the action referred to has happened (or may have happened) in the past.

Je ne crois pas qu'il soit venu.
I do not think [that] he has come.
(I do not think [that] he came.)
(I do not think [that] he did come.)
Il est possible qu'elle l'ait fait.
It is possible [that] she has done it.
(It is possible [that] she did it.)
(It is possible [that] she did do it.)
Je suis content qu'il les ait vus.
I am glad [that] he has seen them.
(I am glad [that] he saw them.)
(I am glad [that] he did see them.)

Remember that the 1st and 2nd persons plural and the 2nd person singular of the present subjunctive of *avoir* and *être* replace the present indicative forms normally used as imperatives, but the 2nd person singular of *avoir* drops its *-s*.

Ayons confiance en lui!
Let's have confidence in him!
Soyons polis!
Let's be polite!
Ayez confiance en moi!
Have confidence in me!
Soyez mon ami!
Be my friend!

(Continued on page 84)

ADDITIONAL INFORMATION

OTHER USES OF THE SUBJUNCTIVE

The subjunctive is mainly used in a subordinate clause following an expression of emotion, possibility, or doubt. It also appears after a phrase containing one of the words below, plus *que*. Notice the word order in the last two French sentences.

qui que, quel (quels, quelle, quelles) que, quelque... que

Qui que ce soit, ne le laissez pas entrer.
Whoever it is (may be), don't let him [come] in.
Quelles que soient vos idées, je ne veux pas y aller.
Whatever your ideas may be, I don't want to go there.
Quelque ambition qu'il ait, il ne nous plaît pas.
Whatever ambition he may have, we don't like him.

The subjunctive may follow a phrase containing a superlative if there is an element of exaggeration.

C'est le meilleur livre que vous puissiez acheter.
It's the best book you can [possibly] buy.
C'est la seule fois qu'elle l'ait fait.
It's the only time she has [ever] done it.
Voilà l'enfant le plus adorable que j'aie jamais vu.
There's the most adorable child I have ever seen.
BUT: *C'est la seule lettre que j'ai écrite aujourd'hui.*
That's the only letter I have written today.

The subjunctive may indicate that the speaker is not sure whether he can find the person or thing he is talking about. The indicative is used when the speaker knows that the person or object exists.

Cet homme veut acheter une maison qui soit près de la gare.
This man wants to buy a house that is (may be) near the station.
Il veut aussi trouver une secrétaire qui comprenne les langues romanes.
He also wants to find a secretary who understands (may understand) Romance languages.
BUT: *Il cherche un hôtel qui est près de la gare.*
He is looking for a hotel which is (in actuality) near the station.
Il veut trouver la secrétaire qui comprend les langues romanes.
He wants to find the secretary who does understand Romance languages.

(Continued on page 84)

EXPLANATIONS

1. *Est-il nécessaire qu'elle **ait fait** cela?* This impersonal expression involving another person in a possible past action (rather than a fact), requires the subjunctive.

2. *C'est bien, pourvu que vous y **soyez allés**.* The conjunction *pourvu que* needs the subjunctive.

3. *Il est vrai que je les **ai vus**.* Since this impersonal phrase states a fact, the indicative mood is correct.

4. *Je crains qu'il **soit venu**.* The subjunctive is required after a statement of emotion and a change of subject.

5. *Elle est contente que vous l'**ayez reçu**.* An emotion involving another person is correctly followed by the subjunctive.

6. *Êtes-vous sûr qu'ils **aient vendu** l'auto?* A doubt affecting someone else requires the subjunctive for a subsequent action.

7. *Nous espérons que tu le lui **as donné**.* The verb *espérer* does not normally take the subjunctive.

8. *Il doit **quitter** Paris demain.* The verb *quitter* is correct when a place is the object.

9. *J'ai **laissé** mes livres chez vous.* *Laisser* means "to leave [behind]."

10. *Vous voulez **partir?*** When the verb has no object, *partir* is needed.

11. *Elle va **partir** de New York.* If the meaning is "to depart [from]," *partir* precedes *de*.

12. *Nous avons **quitté** nos amis ce matin.* A personal direct object requires the verb *quitter*.

Answers

c	1
b	2
d	3
a	4
b	5
c	6
e	7
b	8
a	9
c	10
b	11
c	12

Aie confiance en nous!
Have confidence in us!
Sois sage!
Be good!

Partir, Quitter, Laisser

Partir is an intransitive verb of motion, meaning "to leave" in the sense of "to depart."

Je pars demain.
I leave tomorrow.
Il est déjà parti?
He has already left?

Followed by *de, partir* means "to leave from," or "to depart from."

Nous sommes partis d'Orly.
We left from Orly.
Vous allez partir d'ici?
You are going to leave from here?

Quitter is a transitive verb, which may have as object a person or a place, but not a thing.

Je l'ai quittée il y a une heure.
I left her an hour ago.
Nous allons quitter Caen demain.
We're going to leave Caen tomorrow.

Laisser is a transitive verb, which may have as object a person or a thing, but not a place. It has the meaning "to leave behind" or "to forget."

Elle a laissé son mari à Paris.
She [has] left her husband in Paris.
J'ai laissé mon livre au cinéma.
I left my book at the movies.
Il a laissé son chien chez elle.
He left his dog at her house.
Ils ont laissé leurs photos!
They [have] left their photos!

OTHER TENSES OF THE SUBJUNCTIVE MOOD

Although there are a few other tenses of the subjunctive (which will be presented in Chapter 24), the present and past tenses are adequate for most situations.

AVOIDING THE SUBJUNCTIVE MOOD

Although use of the subjunctive is well defined, it may sometimes be replaced by another construction; this is considered good practice in French. If there is no change of subject following an expression of emotion, often the preposition *de* plus an infinitive may give the meaning simply and clearly.

Elle est heureuse d'être ici.
She is happy that she is here.
(She is happy to be here.)
Ils sont contents de pouvoir vous parler demain.
They are pleased that they can talk to you tomorrow.
(They are pleased to be able to talk to you tomorrow.)

Sometimes a conjunction that normally requires the subjunctive may be changed to a preposition plus a noun.

Vous pouvez le faire sans sa permission.
You can do it without his permitting it.
(You can do it without his permission.)
Il veut partir avant notre arrivée.
He wants to leave before we arrive.
(He wants to leave before our arrival.)

When a change of subject is general, vague, or unessential to the meaning of a sentence, an impersonal phrase may be used, thereby dropping the dependent subject with its subjunctive and replacing it with a preposition (usually *de*) and/or an infinitive.

Il est possible de voir l'exposition maintenant.
We (you, one, they, people) can see the exhibition now.
(It is possible [for us, you, anyone, etc.] to see the exhibition now.)
Il faut le faire tout de suite.
We (you, they, etc.) must do it at once.
(It is necessary [for us, you, etc.] to do it at once.)

OTHER USES OF THE SUBJUNCTIVE OF *Être*

The 3rd person singular of the subjunctive of *être* occurs in several idiomatic expressions.

Il a insisté? Soit!
He insisted? So be it!
Ainsi soit-il!
Amen (at the end of a prayer)!
Elle veut acheter soit (ou) une robe, soit (ou) un chapeau.
She wants to buy either a dress or a hat.

22

VERB SPELLING CHANGES;
FAÇON, MANIÈRE, MOYEN

DIRECTIONS: Complete each of the following sentences by writing the correct form of the present indicative tense on the lines to the right.

1. *Nous _____ (commencer) à comprendre.*

2. *J' _____ (essuyer) la table.*

3. *Elle _____ (acheter) des gants.*

4. *Nous _____ (manger) notre dîner.*

5. *Qu'est-ce qu'ils _____ (employer)?*

6. *Tu _____ (jeter) ces crayons?*

7. *Elle _____ (nettoyer) sa chambre.*

8. *_____ (préférer) -tu ceux-ci?*

9. *Il _____ (suggérer) y aller.*

10. *Ils se _____ (lever) de bonne heure.*

For each of the following sentences, write T (True) on the line to the right if it is correct and write F (False) if it is incorrect.

11. *Par quels moyens a-t-il réussi?*

12. *La manière dans laquelle il le fait est curieuse.*

13. *Sa façon d'agir est absurde.*

14. *Je n'aime pas leur manière de parler.*

15. *Mes façons sont bonnes.*

16. *Votre moyen me déplaît.*

17. *Je n'ai pas les moyens de le faire.*

18. *Il le fait dans une façon incroyable.*

1	
2	
3	
4	
5	
6	
7	
8	
9	
10	
11	
12	
13	
14	
15	
16	
17	
18	

BASIC FACTS

SPELLING CHANGES IN THE PRESENT TENSE

a) *Infinitives ending in -cer, -ger*

Since the *c* and the *g* of these verbs have a soft sound, this sound must be preserved when the following vowel becomes *a, o,* or *u.* (Normally these vowels harden the sound of the consonant, as in *contraire, gabardine,* etc.) The *c* must therefore add a cedilla, and the *g* must be followed by an *e.* In the present indicative tense, this change of spelling occurs in the 1st person plural.

nous commençons	we begin
nous agaçons	we annoy
nous plaçons	we place
nous mangeons	we eat
nous dirigeons	we direct
nous nageons	we swim

b) *Infinitives ending in -oyer, -uyer*

Spelling changes are made for a different reason in the present indicative tense of these verbs. Here the *y* becomes *i* before a mute *e.* The spelling changes occur, therefore, in all the present tense forms except the 1st and 2nd persons plural.

employer	*essuyer*
(to use)	(to clean)
j'emploie	j'essuie
tu emploies	tu essuies
il emploie	il essuie
nous employons	nous essuyons
vous employez	vous essuyez
ils emploient	ils essuient

c) *Infinitives ending in -eler, etc.*

Verbs ending in *-er* preceded by a mute *e* and a single consonant may change their spelling in one of two ways, and these should be noted when the verb is learned. Verbs like *acheter, geler, (se) lever,* etc. add a grave accent to all forms of the present tense except the 1st and 2nd persons plural.

(*Continued on page 88*)

ADDITIONAL INFORMATION

OTHER VERB SPELLING CHANGES

a) *Infinitives ending in -cer, -ger*

The changes required in the 1st person plural of the present indicative tense are also necessary in the present participle and in the imperfect tense, except for the 1st and 2nd persons plural. The reason is the same—to preserve the sound of the original verb form.

INFIN. AND PRES. TENSE	PRES. PART.	IMPERFECT
commencer		
nous commençons	commençant	je commençais
		tu commençais
		il commençait
		nous commencions
		vous commenciez
		ils commençaient
manger		
nous mangeons	mangeant	je mangeais
		tu mangeais
		il mangeait
		nous mangions
		vous mangiez
		ils mangeaient

b) *Infinitives ending in -oyer, -uyer*

Apart from most persons of the present indicative tense, the *whole* of the future and conditional tenses require the same change of *y* to *i.* The present subjunctive has the same changes as the present indicative, but remember that its 1st and 2nd person plural forms end in *-ions* and *-iez.*

INFIN.	PRESENT	FUTURE	CONDIT.
employer	emploie	emploierai	emploierais
	emploies	emploieras	emploierais
	emploie	emploiera	emploierait
	employons	emploierons	emploierions
	employez	emploierez	emploieriez
	emploient	emploieront	emploieraient

c) *Infinitives ending in -eler, -eter, -ever, etc.*

The present subjunctive of these verbs calls for the same spelling changes as the present indicative. The *whole* of the future and conditional tenses also change in the same way.

(*Continued on page 88*)

EXPLANATIONS

1. *Nous **commençons** à comprendre.* Verbs ending in -*cer* need a cedilla before an *a, o,* or *u.*

2. *J'**essuie** la table.* An infinitive ending in -*uyer* changes the *y* to an *i* before a mute *e.*

3. *Elle **achète** des gants.* A mute *e* followed by one consonant and another mute *e* usually requires a grave accent.

4. *Nous **mangeons** notre dîner.* Verbs with a -*ger* infinitive must add an *e* after the *g* before an *a, o,* or *u.*

5. *Qu'est-ce qu'ils **emploient?*** As in Question 2, the *y* changes to an *i* before a mute *e.*

6. *Tu **jettes** ces crayons? Jeter* is a verb that doubles the consonant between two mute *e*'s.

7. *Elle **nettoie** sa chambre.* Like Question 6, the *y* becomes *i* before a mute *e.*

8. ***Préfères**-tu ceux-ci?* An acute accent generally changes to a grave accent on an *e* followed by a single consonant and a mute *e.*

9. *Il **suggère** y aller.* The accent changes here, as in Question 8.

10. *Ils se **lèvent** de bonne heure.* As in Question 3, this verb adds a grave accent on the stressed *e.*

11. *Par quels **moyens** a-t-il réussi? Moyens* translates as the English word "means (ways)."

12. The correct sentence would be: *La manière **dont** il le fait est curieuse.* Because *dans* literally means "inside," it cannot be used here.

13. *Sa **façon** d'agir est absurde.* "Way" here means "fashion" or "method" and requires *façon.*

14. *Je n'aime pas leur **manière** de parler.* This is correct and literally translates as "manner."

15. This sentence should read: *Mes **manières** sont bonnes.* The plural here means "manners" and so requires *manières.*

16. The correct version would be: *Votre **manière** me déplaît.* Again the meaning is "manner."

17. *Je n'ai pas les **moyens** de le faire. Moyens* is correctly translated as "means."

18. This sentence should read: *Il le fait d'une façon incroyable.* As in Question 12, *dans* is incorrect.

Answers	
commen-çons	1
essuie	2
achète	3
mangeons	4
emploient	5
jettes	6
nettoie	7
Préfères	8
suggère	9
lèvent	10
T	11
F	12
T	13
T	14
F	15
F	16
T	17
F	18

j'achète	I buy	
il gèle	it is freezing	
elle se lève	she gets up	

Other verbs, such as *appeler, jeter*, etc., double the consonant when the final *e* becomes mute.

j'appelle	I call
ils jettent	they throw

d) *Infinitives ending in -érer*

Verbs ending in *-er*, where there is already an acute accent on the preceding *e*, change this to a grave accent on all forms of the present tense except the 1st and 2nd persons plural. Examples of these verbs are *préférer* and *suggérer*.

je préfère	I prefer
tu suggères	you (fam.) suggest

Façon, Manière, Moyen

These three words mean "way," but each one has a specific sense. *Façon* literally means "fashion" or "method," and refers largely to action.

Quelle façon de le faire!
What a way of doing it!

Manière more literally translates as "manner" or "air," and indicates appearance.

Sa manière reflète ses doutes.
His manner reflects his doubts.

Moyen, like the English word "means," is often used in the plural.

Avez-vous les moyens d'y réussir?
Have you the means of succeeding [in it]?

INFIN.	PRESENT	FUTURE	CONDIT.
acheter	achète	achèterai	achèterais
geler	gèle	gèlerai	gèlerais
lever	lève	lèverai	lèverais
appeler	appelle	appellerai	appellerais
jeter	jette	jetterai	jetterais

d) *Infinitives ending in -érer*

In the present subjunctive the same accent change is required as in the present indicative. However, there is *no* accent change in the future or conditional tenses.

préférer	préfère	préférerai	préférerais
suggérer	suggère	suggérerai	suggérerais

e) *Infinitives ending in -ayer*

These verbs often have the same spelling changes as those ending in *-oyer* and *-uyer*. However, it is permissible to leave the *y* intact, instead of changing it to *i* before a mute *e*.

essayer	essaie	essaierai	essaierais
(to try)	essaye	essayerai	essayerais
payer	paie	paierai	paierais
(to pay)	paye	payerai	payerais
bégayer	bégaie	bégaierai	bégaierais
(to stammer)	bégaye	bégayerai	bégayerais
effrayer	effraie	effraierai	effraierais
(to frighten)	effraye	effrayerai	effrayerais

Façon, Manière, Moyen

With these words, the preposition *de* is customary.

Sa façon de chanter me plaît.
His (her) way of singing pleases me.
Leur manière de parler est intéressante.
Their way of speaking is interesting.
Vous avez trouvé les moyens de le faire?
You have found the means of doing it?

Notice that the phrase "in which" or "by which" requires the French word *dont*, which of course also means "of which."

La façon dont elle récite est admirable.
The way [in which] she recites is admirable.
La manière dont il a parlé m'offense.
The way [in which] he spoke offends me.
Les moyens dont il a réussi sont douteux.
The means by which he succeeded are dubious.
Les moyens dont ils se sont servis sont louables.
The means that they used (of which they made use) are praiseworthy.

23

CAUSATIVE *FAIRE;*
DEVENIR, ENDROIT, LIEU, PLACE

DIRECTIONS: For each of the following sentences, write T (True) on the line to the right if it is correct and write F (False) if it is incorrect.

1. *Il fait son chien s'asseoir.*

2. *Je fais construire une maison par Paul.*

3. *Nous les faisons suivre.*

4. *Ils les ont fait enregistrés.*

5. *Je lui fais finir son devoir.*

6. *Vous faites les construire.*

7. *Elle fait écrire une lettre à Georges.*

8. *Elles le font lire la lettre.*

9. *Faites-lui venir!*

10. *Ne les faites pas partir!*

Complete each of the following sentences by writing the appropriate word for "place" (*l'endroit, le lieu,* or *la place*) on the numbered lines to the right.

11. *Voilà _____ où l'accident s'est passé.*

12. *Ce n'est ni le temps ni _____.*

13. *Y a-t-il assez de _____ pour moi?* ·

14. *Dans une pièce classique, il faut garder l'unité de _____.*

15. *Cette maison est _____ que je préfère.*

16. *Retenez trois _____ pour ce soir, s'il vous plaît.*

17. *Allez à _____ qu'on vous montrera sur le plan.*

18. *Voici _____ du Lion!*

1	
2	
3	
4	
5	
6	
7	
8	
9	
10	
11	
12	
13	
14	
15	
16	
17	
18	

BASIC FACTS

Causative *Faire*

The verb *faire* in its simple form means "to do" or "to make."

L'avez-vous fait?
Have you done it?
Quand allons-nous le faire?
When are we going to do it?
Elle va faire son devoir.
She is going to do her duty.
Il l'a fait lui-même.
He made it himself.
Elle fait toutes ses robes ici.
She makes all her dresses here.
Je vais faire un effort.
I'm going to make an effort.

Followed by a verb, *faire* translates as "to make" in the sense of "to have something done." Remember that the two verbs must stay together in French.

Ils feront construire une maison.
They will have a house built.
J'ai fait chanter ma fille.
I had my daughter sing.
Elle fait partir son fils.
She makes her son leave.

If the action caused by *faire* involves another person, the preposition *par* is generally used. Notice that the direct object of the action precedes the doer.

Je ferai chanter l'air par ma fille.
I'll have the tune sung by my daughter.
Il fait suivre l'homme par la police.
He has (is having) the man followed by the police.
Elle a fait finir la tâche par son fils.
She had the task (job) finished by her son.

If the object is a pronoun, it precedes both verbs.

Ils la feront construire.
They will have it built.
Je le ferai chanter par ma fille.
I'll have it sung by my daughter.

(*Continued on page 92*)

ADDITIONAL INFORMATION

Causative *Faire*

If the doer of the action caused by *faire* is mentioned, the preposition *à* may replace *par*. Remember that when there are two objects, the doer becomes the indirect object.

Il fait manger l'os à (par) son chien.
He makes (has) his dog eat the bone.
Il le fait manger à (par) son chien.
He makes (has) his dog eat it.
Je ferai couper l'herbe à (par) ce garçon.
I'll have the grass cut by this boy.
Je la ferai couper à (par) ce garçon.
I'll have it cut by this boy.

If both objects are pronouns, their place and order are determined by the normal rules; they must precede *faire*, except in a positive command.

Ils le lui feront écrire.
They will make (have) him write it.
Je vous le ferai lire.
I'll make (have) you read it.
Faites-la-lui construire!
Have (make) him build it!
Ne nous le faites pas finir!
Don't make (have) us finish it!

In the case of a compound tense, the past participle of *faire* remains invariable. It does *not* agree with a preceding direct object of the action it causes because, in this case, the direct object of *faire* is the following verb.

Nous avons fait recommander les lettres.
We [have] had the letters registered.
Nous les avons fait recommander.
We [have] had them registered.
Avez-vous fait enregistrer les bagages?
Did you have the baggage checked?
Oui, je les ai fait enregistrer.
Yes, I [have] had them checked.

Faire may be used with another *faire* to mean "to have something done (made)" or "to have somebody do something."

Vous les avez fait faire? Oui.
You had them done? Yes.
Voilà mes documents. Je veux en faire faire des copies.
There are my documents. I want to have copies made of them.

(*Continued on page 92*)

EXPLANATIONS

1. The correct sentence would be: *Il fait s'asseoir son chien*. The action caused by *faire* must follow it directly.

2. *Je fais construire une maison par Paul*. The preposition *par* introduces the person who is made to do the action.

3. *Nous les faisons suivre*. The pronoun object of the action must precede both verbs.

4. This sentence should read: *Ils les ont fait enregistrer*. An infinitive must follow *faire*.

5. *Je lui fais finir son devoir*. The direct object is *devoir;* therefore, the person performing the action becomes the indirect object.

6. The correct version would be. *Vous les faites construire*. Both verbs in the causative *faire* construction must be together.

7. *Elle fait écrire une lettre à Georges*. The two verbs are together, and the noun objects follow.

8. This sentence should read: *Elles lui font lire la lettre*. Like Question 5, when there are two objects, the doer of the action is the indirect object.

9. The correct sentence would be: *Faites-le venir!* Since there is only one object, it is a direct object. It follows the verb because it is a positive command (imperative).

10. *Ne les faites pas partir!* In a negative command the pronoun precedes the verb.

11. *Voilà l'endroit où l'accident s'est passé*. The word *endroit* indicates a precise spot or place.

12. *Ce n'est ni le temps ni le lieu*. The word *lieu* is used in the same general sense as *temps*.

13. *Y a-t-il assez de place pour moi?* *Place* means "space" or "room."

14. *Dans une pièce classique, il faut garder l'unité de lieu*. *Lieu* is used for place in a more general sense than *endroit*.

15. *Cette maison est l'endroit que je préfère*. Like Question 11, this is a specific place.

16. *Retenez trois places pour ce soir, s'il vous plaît*. *Places* translates as "places" or "seats."

17. *Allez à l'endroit qu'on vous montrera sur le plan*. The meaning here is precise, as in Questions 11 and 15.

18. *Voici la place du Lion!* "Place" in the sense of "public square" requires *place*.

Answers	
F	1
T	2
T	3
F	4
T	5
F	6
T	7
F	8
F	9
T	10
l'endroit	11
le lieu	12
place	13
lieu	14
l'endroit	15
places	16
l'endroit	17
la place	18

Il le fait suivre par la police.
He has him followed by the police.

In a positive command the pronoun follows immediately after *faire,* but in a negative command it precedes the verb as usual.

Faites-les entrer!
Have them come in!
Fais-la manger!
Make her eat!
Ne le faites pas tomber!
Don't make him fall!

Endroit, Lieu, Place

The word *endroit* means a precise place or spot, with definite limits.

Le jardin est un endroit paisible.
The garden is a peaceful place.
Voilà un joli endroit!
There's a pretty spot!

Lieu often indicates place in a more general sense, with no specific limits.

Elles vont à un lieu inconnu.
They are going to an unknown place.
En quel lieu les trouve-t-on?
In what area does one find them?

Place translates as "place (seat)," "room," or "public square."

Voilà deux places!
There are two places (seats)!
Il n'y a pas de place.
There is no room.
Il est dans la place des Vosges.
He is in Vosges Square.

Se Faire, Devenir

In its reflexive form, *faire* means "to become," and thus is a synonym of *devenir.* However, *faire* retains its original sense of "to make," and so implies the idea of "becoming" through one's own efforts. *Devenir,* on the other hand, means "to become (of)" without any special effort.

Elle est devenue malade après la mort de son père.
She became ill after the death of her father.
Que sont-ils devenus? Ils sont en Amérique.
What has become of them? They are in America.
Il est devenu l'image de son grand-père.
He has become the image of his grandfather.
Vous l'avez vu? Oui, il s'est fait médecin.
You saw him? Yes, he has become a doctor.
Elle se fait l'appui de ses parents.
She is becoming the support of her parents.
Il s'était fait le porte-parole des étudiants.
He had become the spokesman of the students.

Endroit, Lieu, Place

Although the meanings of these words may sometimes overlap, there are certain basic differences that should be remembered. *Endroit,* translated as "place" or "spot," also means "passage (in a book)," "side," or "aspect."

Il faut rire au bon endroit.
One must laugh in the right places.
Son discours était très amusant par endroits.
His talk was very amusing in spots (here and there).

Lieu occurs in some adverbial expressions and often in a more general sense. *Avoir lieu* means "to take place."

Je veux le mettre en lieu sûr.
I want to put it in a safe place.
Il l'a entendu dire en haut lieu.
He heard it [said] in high places.
Travaillez au lieu de jouer!
Work instead of playing!
L'élection aura lieu demain.
The election will take place tomorrow.

Place, besides meaning "place," "room," and "public square," also indicates "position," "job," etc.

Il l'a mis en place.	He put it in place.
Je l'ai remise à sa place.	I put her in her place.
Le feriez-vous à ma place?	Would you do it in my place?
Elle a perdu sa place.	She [has] lost her job.

24 OTHER TENSES; *HEURE, TEMPS, FOIS*

DIRECTIONS: Choose the appropriate verb tense listed below for each of the following sentences, and write your answers (a, b, c, d, or e) on the numbered lines to the right.

1. *Napoléon se _____ empereur.*
   a *fut*   b *fût*   c *fit*
   d *fît*   e *fus*

2. *La princesse _____ décidé de rester chez elle.*
   a *eut*   b *eu*   c *fut*
   d *est*   e *était*

3. *Aussitôt qu'il _____ arrivé, il s'assit.*
   a *avait*   b *était*   c *soit*
   d *fut*   e *serait*

4. *Il voulait qu'elle le _____.*
   a *fait*   b *faite*   c *fit*
   d *eût*   e *fît*

5. *A peine _____ -elle fini quand il entra.*
   a *a*   b *eut*   c *aurait*
   d *aura*   e *fut*

6. *Elle lui parla, et il _____.*
   a *sortit*   b *sorţît*   c *sort*
   d *est sorti*   e *sorte*

7. *Ses ancêtres _____ l'honneur en 1549.*
   a *sont reçus*   b *reçoivent*
   c *reçurent*   d *recevaient*
   e *recevront*

Complete each of the following sentences by writing the appropriate form of *l'heure, le temps,* or *la fois* on the numbered lines to the right.

8. *Avez-vous _____ de le voir?*

9. *Il est déjà trois _____.*

10. *Combien de _____ l'avez-vous fait?*

11. *C'est maintenant _____ de votre départ.*

12. *Je vous l'ai déjà dit deux _____.*

13. *Il me reste très peu de _____.*

14. *_____ partie, elle ne reviendra pas.*

93

BASIC FACTS

THE SIMPLE PAST TENSE

This tense has special endings, which are generally added to the basic root of the infinitive. It is sometimes called the past definite or historic past.

donner	*finir*
donnai	finis
donnas	finis
donna	finit
donnâmes	finîmes
donnâtes	finîtes
donnèrent	finirent

vendre	*recevoir*
vendis	reçus
vendis	reçus
vendit	reçut
vendîmes	reçûmes
vendîtes	reçûtes
vendirent	reçurent

Remember that there are always some irregular verbs. The simple past tense replaces the compound past when relating a single action such as a historic event, or in a literary work such as a novel. It is *not* used in conversation or letter writing.

> *La guerre éclata en 1618.*
> The war broke out in 1618.
> *Dickens raconta l'histoire de sa vie dans David Copperfield.*
> Dickens told the story of his life in *David Copperfield.*

THE PAST ANTERIOR TENSE

The past anterior is formed from the simple past of *avoir* or *être* plus a past participle.

avoir	*être*
eus	fus
eus	fus
eut	fut
eûmes	fûmes
eûtes	fûtes
eurent	furent

(Continued on page 96)

ADDITIONAL INFORMATION

THE IMPERFECT SUBJUNCTIVE OF *Avoir* AND *Être*

avoir	*être*
eusse	fusse
eusses	fusses
eût	fût
eussions	fussions
eussiez	fussiez
eussent	fussent

This tense is used in a dependent clause in past time when the action has not yet happened. The normal rules for use of the subjunctive must be observed.

> *Ses ennemis voulaient qu'il fût prisonnier.*
> His enemies wished [that] he were a prisoner.
> *Le roi ordonna qu'ils eussent confiance en lui.*
> The king ordered them to have (that they should have) confidence in him.

The imperfect subjunctive may also appear in non-literary use if the dependent action has not yet happened.

> *Ses enfants voulaient qu'il mourût.*
> His children wanted him to die.
> *Il était possible qu'il arrivât.*
> It was possible [that] he might arrive.

IRREGULAR FORMS OF THE SIMPLE PAST TENSE

As usual, the 1st conjugation verbs ending in *-er* are quite regular. The 2nd conjugation's main irregular verbs in this tense are:

INFIN.	SIMPLE PAST	IMPERF. SUBJ.
courir	courus	courusse
mourir	mourus	mourusse
venir	vins	vinsse

The common irregular verbs of the 3rd conjugation are as follows:

conduire	conduisis	conduisisse
craindre	craignis	craignisse
dire	dis	disse
écrire	écrivis	écrivisse
faire	fis	fisse
mettre	mis	misse
prendre	pris	prisse

Others of this conjugation change the vowel to a *u:*

connaître	connus	connusse
croire	crus	crusse
lire	lus	lusse
plaire	plus	plusse

(Continued on page 96)

EXPLANATIONS

1. *Napoléon se **fit** empereur.* The simple past tense is necessary for a historic event.

2. *La princesse **eut** décidé de rester chez elle.* For literary narrative style, the past anterior is preferred to the pluperfect tense.

3. *Aussitôt qu'il **fut** arrivé, il s'assit.* The past anterior is required with a simple past tense that follows.

4. *Il voulait qu'elle le **fît.*** The imperfect subjunctive is sometimes used for a subordinate action in past time.

5. *A peine **eut**-elle fini quand il entra.* Like Question 3, the past anterior accompanies a simple past tense.

6. *Elle lui parla, et il **sortit.*** Both actions are in the simple past literary tense.

7. *Ses ancêtres **reçurent** l'honneur en 1549.* The simple past tense is necessary when referring to a historic date.

8. *Avez-vous **le temps** de le voir? Temps* is translated as "time" in a general, non-specific sense.

9. *Il est déjà trois **heures.*** Time of day requires the word *heure*.

10. *Combien de **fois** l'avez-vous fait?* "Times" (meaning "occasions") is *fois* in French.

11. *C'est maintenant **l'heure** de votre départ. Heure* is used for a specific time.

12. *Je vous l'ai déjà dit deux **fois.*** As with Question 10, "times" in this example means "occasions."

13. *Il me reste très peu de **temps.*** "Time" in the general sense is *temps,* as in Question 8.

14. ***Une fois** partie, elle ne reviendra pas.* "Once," meaning "one time (occasion)," requires *fois*.

Answers

c	1
a	2
d	3
e	4
b	5
a	6
c	7
le temps	8
heures	9
fois	10
l'heure	11
fois	12
temps	13
Une fois	14

The past anterior replaces the pluperfect tense for historic or literary use.

> *La guerre eut éclaté en 1618.*
> The war had broken out in 1618.
> *Le roi fut parti avant leur mort.*
> The king had left before their death.

This tense may combine with a simple past, in the same way as a pluperfect with a compound past.

> *Elle eut déjà éclaté quand il mourut.*
> It had already broken out when he died.

THE IMPERFECT SUBJUNCTIVE

The stem of the imperfect subjunctive is based upon the 2nd person singular of the simple past tense. This tense may replace the past subjunctive in literary or historic style.

donner	*finir*
donnasse	finisse
donnasses	finisses
donnât	finît
donnassions	finissions
donnassiez	finissiez
donnassent	finissent

vendre	*recevoir*
vendisse	reçusse
vendisses	reçusses
vendît	reçût
vendissions	reçussions
vendissiez	reçussiez
vendissent	reçussent

> *Il voulait qu'elle entrât.*
> He wanted her to enter.
> *Le général demanda qu'il le finît.*
> The general demanded [that] he finish it.

Heure, Temps, Fois

Heure indicates a precise time of day; *temps* is translated as "time" in general, and *fois* means "occasion."

Most simple past tense forms of the 4th conjugation contract the stem except *falloir* (*[il] fallut, [il] fallût*), *vouloir* (*voulus, voulusse*), and *valoir* (*valus, valusse*).

INFIN.	SIMPLE PAST	IMPERF. SUBJ.
devoir	dus	dusse
pleuvoir	(il) plut	(il) plût
pouvoir	pus	pusse
savoir	sus	susse
BUT: voir	vis	visse

THE PLUPERFECT SUBJUNCTIVE

Occasionally a further tense is needed for the subjunctive; it is composed of the imperfect subjunctive of *avoir* or *être* plus a past participle.

> *Il ne croyait pas que les soldats l'eussent dit.*
> He did not believe [that] the soldiers had said it.
> *Il était possible que l'ennemi fût arrivé.*
> It was possible [that] the enemy had arrived.

The pluperfect subjunctive is sometimes used in literary style instead of the indicative past conditional.

> *Elle eût préféré se marier avec un médecin.*
> (*Elle aurait préféré...*)
> She would have preferred to marry a doctor.

Heure, Temps, Fois

A precise time of day requires the word *heure*.

> *Il est une heure et demie.*
> It is 1:30.
> *A quelle heure partez-vous?*
> [At] what time are you leaving?
> *Le train est à l'heure.*
> The train is on time (schedule).

However, notice that when *demi* precedes the word *heure* it remains invariable.

> *Il y a une demi-heure d'attente.*
> There is a half-hour's wait.

Heure is also used in some idiomatic expressions.

> *Elle se lève de bonne heure.*
> She gets up early.
> *Vous avez fini? A la bonne heure!*
> You have finished? Splendid (excellent, wonderful)!

Temps means "time" in a more general sense.

> *Je n'ai pas le temps d'y aller.*
> I haven't the time to go there.
> *Vous êtes arrivé juste à temps.*
> You arrived just in time.

Fois is translated as "occasion."

> *Il l'a fait une fois, deux fois, trois fois.*
> He did it once, twice, three times.

VERBS WITH PREPOSITIONS;
FAUTE, DÉFAUT, ERREUR

SELF-TEST

DIRECTIONS: For each of the following sentences, write T (True) on the line to the right if it is correct and write F (False) if it is incorrect.

1. *J'ai oublié d'écrire la lettre.*

2. *Il hésite de le faire.*

3. *Nous nous amusons à nager.*

4. *Il obéit sa mère.*

5. *Je lui ai invité à dîner.*

6. *Vous essaierez de le faire?*

7. *Elle pense à ses amis.*

8. *Ils n'ont pas le temps à voyager.*

9. *Vous jouez du piano?*

10. *Il a décidé à venir.*

Complete each of the following sentences by writing the appropriate form of the word *défaut*, *erreur*, or *faute* (meaning "fault" or "mistake") on the numbered lines to the right.

11. *Il est gentil; il a peu de* _____.

12. *Vous pensez cela? Quelle* _____!

13. *Il y a des* _____ *dans son caractère.*

14. *Ils ont volé et menti? Ce sont des* _____ *graves.*

15. *Combien de* _____ *sur cette page!*

16. *Il faut pardonner les* _____ *de la jeunesse.*

17. *Ce n'est pas vrai! Vour êtes dans* _____.

1	
2	
3	
4	
5	
6	
7	
8	
9	
10	
11	
12	
13	
14	
15	
16	
17	

BASIC FACTS

VERBS REQUIRING *à*

à + INFIN.	*à* + NOUN
apprendre	assister
arriver	déplaire
commencer	désobéir
consentir	équivaloir
hésiter	obéir
inviter	plaire
renoncer	ressembler
réussir	satisfaire
s'amuser	subvenir
se mettre	manquer

Il a consenti à venir.
He consented to come.
Je réussis à le faire.
I succeed in doing it.
Il ressemble à son père.
He resembles his father.
Elle lui plaît.
She pleases him.

Since many of these verbs are transitive in English, it is often helpful to paraphrase them.

He has a resemblance **to** his father.
She is pleasing **to** him.

Notice the special meaning of some verbs in French.

assister à	to attend, be present at
subvenir à	to provide for
manquer à	to be missed by

VERBS REQUIRING *de*

de + INFIN.	*de* + NOUN
accepter	douter
cesser	se douter
essayer	s'évader
finir	se servir
oublier	
refuser	
se dépêcher	
tâcher	
tenter	
venir	

Although *à* together with an infinitive may indicate an action to be done,

(*Continued on page 100*)

ADDITIONAL INFORMATION

VERBS FOLLOWED BY *à* OR *de*

à + INFIN.	*de* + INFIN.
manquer	ne pas manquer
passer le temps	avoir le temps
se décider	décider

Nous avons manqué à lui écrire.
We failed to write to him (her).
Ne manquez pas de le faire!
Don't fail to do it!
Il passe son temps à étudier.
He spends his time studying.
Elle a le temps de visiter le musée.
She has the time to visit the museum.
Je me suis décidé(e) à y aller.
I [have] decided to go there.
Avez-vous décidé de lire ce roman?
Have you decided to read that novel?

Some verbs have a similar duality with nouns.

à + NOUN	*de* + NOUN
échapper	s'échapper
jouer	jouer
penser	penser

Il a échappé à son travail.
He has escaped [from] his work.
L'oiseau s'est échappé de sa cage.
The bird escaped from his cage.
Vous jouez au tennis?
You play tennis?
Moi, je joue du violin.
I play the violin.
A quoi pensez-vous?
What are you thinking about?
Que pensent-ils de cette pièce?
What do they think of this play?

Notice also *servir à* (+ infin.) and *servir de* (+ noun).

Cette machine sert à couper l'herbe.
That machine serves to cut the grass.
Ce banc sert quelquefois de table.
This bench sometimes serves as a table.

The verb *manquer* followed by *à* (+ noun) means "to be missed by," and is the reverse of the English construction.

Vous manquez terriblement à vos amis.
Your friends miss you terribly!

VERBS + *à* + *de*

These verbs may be classed largely as verbs of communication. They take *à* before the personal object and *de* before the action.

(*Continued on page 100*)

EXPLANATIONS

1. *J'ai oublié d'écrire la lettre. Oublier* requires *de* before an infinitive. The implication is that the forgetter is going away from the action.

2. This sentence should read: *Il hésite à le faire. Hésiter* takes *à* when followed by an infinitive of an action to be performed by the subject.

3. *Nous nous amusons à nager.* The preposition *à* is correct with an infinitive of action.

4. The correct sentence would be: *Il obéit à sa mère.* The sense is that he gives obedience *to* his mother.

5. This sentence should read: *Je l'ai invité à dîner.* The pronoun is the direct object of the verb.

6. *Vous essaierez de le faire? Essayer* takes *de,* although the sense of action is positive.

7. *Elle pense à ses amis.* The preposition *à* here means "about."

8. The correct version would be: *Ils n'ont pas le temps de voyager.* Many verbal phrases with a noun require *de* before an infinitive.

9. *Vous jouez du piano? Jouer* takes *de* when referring to a musical instrument.

10. This sentence should read: *Il a décidé de venir. Décider* requires *de;* this distinguishes it from *se décider à.*

11. *Il est gentil; il a peu de défauts.* Faults of character require the French word *défauts.*

12. *Vous pensez cela? Quelle erreur!* A mistake in thought or judgment is *erreur.*

13. *Il y a des défauts dans son caractère.* Like Question 11, faults of character are *défauts.*

14. *Ils ont volé et menti? Ce sont des fautes graves. Faute* means faults of action.

15. *Combien de fautes sur cette page!* Like Question 14, *fautes* refers to faults committed.

16. *Il faut pardonner les erreurs de la jeunesse.* Faults in thought and judgment are *erreurs.*

17. *Ce n'est pas vrai! Vous êtes dans l'erreur. Erreur* again means a mental error.

Answers	
T	1
F	2
T	3
F	4
F	5
T	6
T	7
F	8
T	9
F	10
défauts	11
erreur	12
défauts	13
fautes	14
fautes	15
erreurs	16
l'erreur	17

and *de* may mean a going away *from* an action, there are exceptions in both groups.

> *Je renonce à y aller.*
> I give up [the idea of] going there.
> *Il tâche de comprendre.*
> He tries to understand.

Notice the following idiomatic expressions:

douter de	to doubt
se douter de	to suspect
se servir de	to make use of, help oneself to
venir de	to have just

> *Elle doute de son amitié.*
> She doubts (has doubts about) his friendship.
> *Je me doute de lui.*
> I suspect him.
> *Servez-vous!*
> Help yourself!
> *Il vient d'arriver.*
> He has just arrived.

Faute, Défaut, Erreur

The word *faute* usually denotes a visible fault or a fault in action.

> *C'est une faute d'orthographe.*
> That's a spelling mistake.
> *Ce n'est pas [de] ma faute.*
> It's not my fault.

Défaut generally implies an intangible defect or lack.

> *C'est un défaut de courage.*
> It's a lack of courage.
> *Jugement par défaut...*
> Judgment by default . . .

Erreur means "fault," "mistake," or "blunder (in comprehension)."

> *C'est une erreur de date.*
> It's a mistake in date.
> *Je l'ai fait par erreur.*
> I did it by mistake.
> *Il m'a tiré d'erreur.*
> He undeceived me.

défendre	demander	dire
ordonner	pardonner	permettre
persuader	reprocher	téléphoner

> *Je lui défends de le faire.*
> I forbid him to do it.
> *Elle leur pardonne d'avoir menti.*
> She forgives them for lying.
> *J'ai persuadé à ma mère d'y aller.*
> I persuaded my mother to go there.

Notice that *enseigner* is followed by *à* in both cases.

> *Il enseigne aux enfants à écrire.*
> He teaches the children to write.

BUT: *Il enseigne les enfants.*

OTHER VERBS WITH VARIABLE CONSTRUCTIONS

échouer à (or dans) + noun

réussir à (or dans) + noun

renoncer à + noun (or no preposition)

NOTE: The preposition *dans* is often preferred to *à*.

> *Il a échoué à (dans) son examen.*
> He has failed his exam.
> *J'ai réussi à (dans) mon travail.*
> I succeeded in my work.
> *Elle a renoncé (à) sa religion.*
> She renounced her religion.

VERBS WITH NO PREPOSITION BEFORE A NOUN

attendre	to wait for	*écouter*	to listen to
chercher	to look for	*payer*	to pay for
demander	to ask for	*regarder*	to look at

> *J'attends mon ami(e).* I'm waiting for my friend.
> *Il a demandé le livre.* He asked for the book.

Faute, Défaut, Erreur

There are several idiomatic uses for each of these words.

Faute

> *Il faut le faire sans faute.*
> It must be done without fail.
> *Faute de mieux, elle l'a accepté.*
> For want of something better, she accepted it.
> *C'est lui qui est en faute, et c'est une faute grave.*
> It is he who is at fault, and it's a serious offense.

Défaut

> *L'argent lui fait défaut.* His money is giving out.
> *Ils m'ont mis en défaut.* They put me on the wrong track.[1]
> *On les a pris en défaut.* They were caught out.

Erreur

> *Vous êtes dans l'erreur.*
> You are under a misapprehension.
> *J'ai commis une erreur.*
> I made a slip.

Final Examination

Index

FINAL EXAMINATION Part I

Questions

DIRECTIONS: Write your answers on a separate sheet of paper. To check your answers, turn to page 104. Study the explanations for any questions you missed.

1. Make the following sentences plural:
   a *Le bateau de mon frère est beau.*
   b *Celui que je préfère est le premier.*
   c *Elle est arrivée? Pas que je sache.*

2. Make the following sentences feminine:
   a *Cet enfant est paresseux.*
   b *Ils sont gentils, mais vieux.*
   c *Il est médecin, et très fier.*

3. Change the following adjectives into adverbs:
   a *net*   b *affreux*   c *vite*

4. Add the correct prepositions to the following verbs:
   a *refuser* _____   b *recommencer* _____
   c *hésiter* _____   d *tâcher* _____

5. Give the French for:
   a he will make
   b I would come
   c they have died

6. Supply the correct prepositions:
   a *Il parlait_____(in) une voix basse.*
   b *C'est l'homme_____(with) cheveux roux.*
   c *Il habite_____(in) Canada.*

7. Insert the words "may" or "must not" where appropriate:
   a French sentences _____ use two futures.
   b *Si* (if) _____ directly precede a future tense.
   c The conditional _____ show obligation.

8. Translate into French:
   The books he had bought were French.

9. Fill in the correct verb tense:
   a *S'il* _____(were) *vous, il le* _____ (would see).

b *Je ne suis pas sûr qu'il* _____(is coming).
   c *Tous les jours* _____(he would go) *la voir.*

10. Translate into French:
    a What I want is a good meal.
    b Which of these books is yours?
    c Do you like this dress or that one?

11. Change the following sentence so that the subjunctive mood is not used:
    Il est content qu'elle soit arrivée.

12. Fill in the correct adverbial forms:
    a *Elle parle* _____(politely).
    b *Ils jouent* _____(constantly).
    c *Jean le fait* _____(worse) *que Louis.*

13. Complete the following sentences using *dont* where correct:
    a *Voilà l'homme* _____(whose wife) *je connais.*
    b *C'est elle* _____(whose courage) *est grand.*
    c *C'est une femme* _____(to whose son) *j'ai parlé.*

14. Give the French for:
    a you had taken
    b I opened
    c (that) he may go (subjunctive)

15. Rewrite the following sentence using the French past infinitive:
    Je suis content de la voir.

16. Complete:
    Je n'ai pas _____(the time) *de retenir* _____ (seats).

17. Insert the correct disjunctive pronouns:
    a _____(I), *je le sais. Et* _____(you) (fam. sing.)?
    b _____(They), *ils vont venir, mais* _____ (he), *non.*
    c _____(We), *nous le voulons. Et* _____ (they, f.)?

18. Use *devoir* or *falloir* in the following:
    a _____(You should) *le savoir.*
    b _____(We must) *aller voir ce musée.*
    c _____(I was to) *lui écrire hier.*

19. Is the following word order correct? If not, rewrite it correctly.
    Peut-être il veut le faire.

20. Complete the following sentences:
    a *Où les avez-vous* _____(left)?
    b *Il va* _____(to leave) *Paris demain.*
    c *Ils* _____(left) *hier.*

21. Give the French for:
    a we shall send
    b she would have understood
    c they had gone away

22. Insert the correct pronoun object:
    a *Je vais* _____ *téléphoner.* (her)
    b *Allons* _____ *chercher.* (for him)
    c *Demandez-* _____ *de venir.* (them)

23. The same preposition for "in" is used with the French names for three of the seasons. This preposition is ____. The exception and its preposition are _____.

24. Translate into French:
    After finishing work, he went out.

25. Insert the correct interrogatives:
    a _____(Whom) *avez-vous vu?*
    b _____(What) *s'est passé?*
    c _____(Which ones, m.) *préférez-vous?*

26. Complete the following sentences:
    a *Il est* ____(in) *Portugal.*
    b *Nice se trouve* _____(in the southeast).
    c *La France est* ____(in) *Europe.*

27. Make the following past participle agree, if necessary:
    Ils se sont parlé.

28. Complete the following sentences:
    a _____(I have just) *finir.*
    b _____(He'd been waiting) *depuis une heure.*
    c *Elle a été à Paris* _____(for) *un mois.*

29. Give the French for:
    a she was born
    b I had received
    c they would be able

30. Insert the correct past participles:
    a *Ils se sont* _____(regarder).
    b *Elle s'est* _____(acheter) *des livres.*
    c *Nous nous sommes* _____(écrire).

31. Supply the French words for:
    a *J'ai* _____(some) *bons vins.*
    b *Il n'a* _____(any) *idée.*
    c *Voilà* _____(some) *bon potage!*

32. Translate into French:
    He didn't want to think about anything.

33. Make the following negative:
    a *Je l'ai vu* _____(never).
    b *Il fait* _____(nothing).
    c *Ils ont aimé* _____(nobody).

34. Supply the correct verb forms for:
    a *Sors avant qu'elle* _____(venir).
    b *Quand il* _____(arriver), *je le verrai.*
    c *Je veux qu'ils le* _____(faire).

35. Complete the following sentences:
    a *Voici mon livre. Où est* _____(yours)?
    b *Ma maison est près de* _____(theirs).
    c *Vos fleurs et* _____(mine) *sont là.*

36. Complete the following:
    a It is 4:40 P.M.
    b I've eaten two-thirds of it.
    c This is the tenth page.

37. Put the following sentence into the active voice:
    Paul a été sauvé par Jean.

EXPLANATIONS

1. a   *Les bateaux de mes frères sont beaux.*
   b   ***Ceux** que nous préférons sont les premiers.*
   c   *Elles sont arrivées? Pas que nous **sachions.***
   Important points are in boldface type.

2. a   *Cette enfant est paresseuse.*
   b   *Elles sont gentilles, mais vieilles.*
   c   *Elle est médecin, et très fière.*

3. a   *nettement*   b   *affreusement*   c   *vite*
   A French adverb is regularly formed by adding *-ment* to the feminine adjective unless the masculine already ends in a vowel. *Vite* is an exception.

4. a   *refuser de*   b   *recommencer à*
   c   *hésiter à*   d   *tâcher de*

5. a   *il **fera***
   b   *je **viendrais***
   c   *ils **sont morts***
   Important points are in boldface type.

6. a   *Il parlait d'une voix basse.*
   b   *C'est l'homme **aux** cheveux roux.*
   c   *Il habite **au** Canada.*

7. a   French sentences **may** use two futures (if both actions are in future time).
   b   *Si* (if) **must not** directly precede a future tense.
   c   The conditional **must not** show obligation (*devoir* or *falloir* must be used).

8. *Les livres qu'il avait achetés étaient français.* Notice the *s* on *achetés*, agreeing with the preceding direct object *qu'*.

9. a   *S'il **était** vous, il le **verrait.***
   b   *Je ne suis pas sûr qu'il **vienne.***
   c   *Tous les jours il **allait** la voir.*
   In *a*, *si* (meaning "if") takes the imperfect when followed by the conditional. In *b*, the uncertainty in the main statement requires the subjunctive for the following verb. In *c*, the imperfect expresses an action repeated every day.

10. a   ***Ce que** je veux, c'est un bon repas.*
    b   ***Lequel** de ces livres est le vôtre (**à vous**)?*
    c   *Aimez-vous cette robe-**ci** ou celle-**là**?*
    In *a*, the *ce* refers back to an idea previously mentioned.

11. *Il est content **de la voir** (or Il est content **de son arrivée**).* The subjunctive mood may sometimes be avoided by using a preposition plus an infinitive, a preposition plus a noun, or dropping a vague dependent subject.

12. a   *Elle parle **poliment.***
    b   *Ils jouent **constamment.***
    c   *Jean le fait **pis** que Louis.*
    In *c*, *pis* is the adverbial form of the adjective *pire*.

13. a   *Voilà l'homme **dont** je connais **la femme.*** As the noun object of the verb, *la femme* must follow it.
    b   *C'est elle **dont le courage** (**le courage de laquelle**) est grand.* As the subject of *est*, *courage* precedes.
    c   *C'est une femme **au fils de qui** (**de laquelle**) j'ai parlé.* *Dont* must not be used with another preposition.

14. a   *vous aviez **pris***
    b   *j'ai **ouvert***
    c   *(qu')il **aille***

15. *Je suis content de **l'avoir vue.*** The French past infinitive is formed from *avoir* or *être* plus a past participle.

16. *Je n'ai pas **le temps** de retenir des places.*

17. a   ***Moi,** je le sais. Et **toi**?*
    b   ***Eux,** ils vont venir, mais **lui,** non.*
    c   ***Nous,** nous le voulons. Et **elles**?*

18. a   *Vous **devriez** le savoir.* Personal obligation needs *devoir,* and "should" or "ought" requires the conditional tense.
    b   *Il **faut** aller voir ce musée.* This is an impersonal obligation. The personal pronoun

is omitted when an infinitive follows. An alternative is a subjunctive clause: *Il faut que nous allions...*

c   *Je devais lui écrire hier.* "I was [supposed] to" needs devoir.

19. *Peut-être veut-il le faire* (or *Il veut le faire, peut-être*). In French, inversion of subject and verb occurs after *aussi* (therefore), *peut-être,* or *à peine;* after spoken words; or when the subjects of both verbs are nouns.

20. a   *Où les avez-vous laissés?*
    b   *Il va quitter Paris demain.*
    c   *Ils sont partis hier.*

21. a   *nous enverrons*
    b   *elle aurait compris*
    c   *ils s'en étaient allés*

22. a   *Je vais lui téléphoner.*
    b   *Allons le chercher.*
    c   *Demandez-leur de venir.*
    Examples *a* and *c* have verbs of communication, which take an indirect object.

23. *en*
    au printemps

24. *Après avoir fini le travail, il est sorti.* The past infinitive is required when the first action is already completed.

25. a   *Qui avez-vous vu?*
    b   *Qu'est-ce qui s'est passé?*
    c   *Lesquels préférez-vous?*

26. a   *Il est au Portugal.*
    b   *Nice se trouve au sud-est.*
    c   *La France est en Europe.*

27. *Ils se sont parlé* is correct. In a reflexive verb, the past participle agrees with a preceding *direct* object pronoun, not with an indirect object.

28. a   *Je viens de finir.* An action just completed is in the present tense of the idiomatic *venir de.*
    b   *Il attendait depuis une heure. Depuis* uses

the imperfect for duration of time in the past when the action is still going on.

c   *Elle a été à Paris pendant un mois.* "For" in past time is *pendant* when the action is completed.

29. a   *elle est née*
    b   *j'avais reçu*
    c   *ils pourraient*

30. a   *Ils se sont regardés.* The *s* agrees with direct object *se.*
    b   *Elle s'est acheté des livres.* The direct object is *livres,* not *s'.*
    c   *Nous nous sommes écrit.* The second *nous* is an indirect object.

31. a   *J'ai de bons vins.* A plural adjective before a noun uses *de.*
    b   *Il n'a aucune idée* (or *Il n'a pas d'idée*).
    c   *Voilà du bon potage!* A singular adjective preceding a noun uses the normal partitive.

32. *Il ne voulait penser à rien.* "To think about" is *penser à.*

33. a   *Je ne l'ai jamais vu.*
    b   *Il ne fait rien.*
    c   *Ils n'ont aimé personne.*
    Personne, like *aucun* and *que* are exceptions; they follow a past participle.

34. a   *Sors avant qu'elle [ne] vienne.*
    b   *Quand il arrivera, je le verrai.*
    c   *Je veux qu'ils le fassent.*
    In *a, ne* is optional.

35. a   *Voici mon livre. Où est le vôtre (le tien)?*
    b   *Ma maison est près de la leur.*
    c   *Vos fleurs et les miennes sont là.*

36. a   *Il est cinq heures moins vingt de l'après-midi.*
    b   *J'en ai mangé deux tiers.*
    c   *C'est la dixième page.*

37. *Jean a sauvé Paul.* The passive voice may be avoided by using the pronouns *on* or *se* and an active verb, or by reversing the sentence when the doer of the action is mentioned.

FINAL EXAMINATION Part II

DIRECTIONS: Translate the following sentences into French on a separate sheet of paper. Then turn to page 108 and compare your translations with the ones given there.

1. Catherine is a darling little girl, with brown hair and green eyes. She is a year and a half old, and is very active.

2. Catherine's mother has pretty brown hair, and is tall and slim. Her father has blue eyes. He is an artist and he likes to play football.

3. Their cat is called Tammy; she catches mice, and sometimes a bird. That is naughty.

4. They used to live near the sea, and they would visit Catherine's grandmother, who had a pretty pink house surrounded by trees.

5. Two days ago, there was an accident at the corner of the street. An old man, who had just come out of a big store, was killed by a car.

6. There were many people waiting for the arrival of the police and looking at the place at which the accident had taken place.

7. The following day, the woman, whose car had caused the man's death and who realized her responsibility towards his relatives, visited them and offered them her assistance.

8. They refused it, but thanked her politely and told her they were grateful but that they could never accept anything.

9. "Robert," his mother said to him, "come quickly! I want you to clean your room and your brother's at once."

10. "I don't want to," he replied. "Please let me go and play with John and Peter. They're waiting for me."

11. "But look at your room," she insisted. "It is dirty and you must clean it soon, certainly before your father arrives."

12. "After cleaning it," his mother continued, "you may go to John's; but tell them you have to be back before six-thirty."

13. It was warm, the sun was shining, and there were a few small white clouds in the blue sky.

14. There was nobody on the beach, but a large red boat in the water was rapidly approaching the land.

15. Sitting on a rock, George was watching it with interest. Two men came out of it when the boat touched the sand.

16. He thought he had seen them earlier, when he and a friend of his had discovered a cave in the rocks, in which they had found several old boxes and pieces of iron.

17. Henry and Paul met in the park at noon before going to have lunch together.

18. "Let's go to Maxim's," suggested Henry. "O.K.," Paul replied, "but I'm very hungry, and it's rather expensive at Maxim's."

19. "Well, we can go to another restaurant; it doesn't matter," Henry said. "Perhaps it would be better to go to the one you know."

20. "When we have finished our meal, let's have our coffee at the little 'bistro' near the hotel. That's said to be quite interesting because of the famous people who go to it."

21. "What a pretty dress, Mary! Is it the one you had your sister make?"

22. "Yes, it's a dress I can wear anywhere, at any time of day. Will you come with me to the concert tonight?"

23. "No, I can't. I haven't the time to attend a concert this week, because next week I have to go to Paris to study."

24. "Oh, you have forgotten to give me your new address. Will you give it to me now?"

25. Michael had been studying for a year at the University of Caen in Normandy.

26. He had seen many beautiful things, old churches, interesting towns, and magnificent paintings.

27. He thought Normandy was one of the most picturesque provinces he had ever seen, with its ancient houses and charming ports.

28. Every day he would go to his favorite little café near the old castle to meet his friends.

29. Josephine, whose grandfather was French, went to Paris by plane with her cousin Sylvia to spend the month of April with friends there.

30. They visited the most famous museums, the beautiful gardens, and the superb monuments such as the Eiffel Tower.

31. One day her cousin was given tickets for the Comédie Française, and they and some of their friends saw one of Molière's plays.

32. They were very sorry to leave at the end of the month, having appreciated the good meals and the wonderful experiences they had had.

33. Susan and her boyfriend Paul were American students at a big university.

34. They had been learning French for some years so as to be able to go to France with their friends.

35. After their visit Paul said: "If I had only known how much nicer it is to be able to speak the language of a country, I would have studied even more."

36. "I am not sure," added Susan, "that all students realized the importance their visit had for international understanding."

37. "I shall always be glad," continued Susan, "that we had the opportunity to go and see the way others live and begin to understand their culture."

EXPLANATIONS

1. *Catherine est une petite fille adorable (mignonne), aux cheveux bruns et aux yeux verts. Elle a un an et demi, et elle est très active.*

2. *La mère de Catherine a les cheveux bruns et jolis, et elle est grande et svelte (mince). Son père a les yeux bleus. Il est artiste (c'est un artiste), et il aime jouer au football.*

3. *Leur chatte s'appelle Tammy; elle attrape des souris, et quelquefois un oiseau. C'est méchant.*

4. *Ils habitaient (demeuraient, vivaient) près de la mer, et ils faisaient (rendaient) visite à la grand-mère de Jeannette, qui avait une jolie maison rose entourée d'arbres.*

5. *Il y a deux jours, il y a eu un accident au coin de la rue. Un vieux (vieillard, vieil homme), qui venait de sortir d'un grand magasin, a été tué par une auto (voiture). (Alternative: Une auto a tué un vieux qui...)*

6. *Il y avait beaucoup de gens qui attendaient l'arrivée de la police et regardaient l'endroit où l'accident avait eu lieu.*

7. *Le lendemain, la femme dont l'auto avait tué (causé la mort de) l'homme et qui se rendait compte de sa responsabilité envers ses parents, leur a rendu (fait) visite et leur a offert son aide.*

8. *Ils l'ont refusée, mais ils l'ont remerciée poliment et lui ont dit qu'ils étaient reconnaissants mais qu'ils ne pourraient jamais rien accepter.*

9. *« Robert, lui a dit sa mère, viens vite! Je veux que tu nettoies ta chambre et celle de ton frère tout de suite. »*

10. *« Je ne veux pas », a-t-il répondu. « S'il te plaît, laisse-moi aller jouer avec Jean et Pierre. Ils m'attendent. »*

11. *« Mais regarde ta chambre », a-t-elle insisté. « Elle est sale et tu dois la nettoyer bientôt, certainement avant l'arrivée de ton père (avant que ton père [n'] arrive). »*

12. *« Après l'avoir nettoyée, a continué sa mère, tu peux aller chez Jean, mais dis-leur qu'il faut que tu sois de retour avant six heures et demie. »*

13. *Il faisait chaud, le soleil brillait, et il y avait quelques petits nuages blancs au ciel bleu.*

14. *Il n'y avait personne sur la plage, mais un grand bateau rouge dans l'eau s'approchait rapidement de la terre.*

15. *Assis sur un rocher, Georges le regardait avec intérêt. Deux hommes en sont sortis quand le bateau a touché le sable.*

16. *Il pensait qu'il les avait vus plus tôt, quand lui et un de ses amis avaient découvert une cave dans les rochers, où (dans laquelle) ils avaient trouvé plusieurs vieilles boîtes et des morceaux de fer.*

17. *Henri et Paul se sont retrouvés (rencontrés) dans le parc à midi avant d'aller déjeuner ensemble.*

18. *« Allons chez Maxim », a suggéré Henri. « Bon, a répondu Paul, mais j'ai très faim, et c'est assez cher chez Maxim. »*

19. *« Eh bien, nous pouvons aller à un autre restaurant; n'importe, a dit Henri. Peut-être vaudrait-il mieux aller à celui que vous connaissez (tu connais). »*

20. *« Quand nous aurons terminé (fini) notre repas, prenons notre café au petit « bistro » près de l'hôtel. On dit que c'est assez intéressant à cause des gens célèbres qui y vont. »*

21. « *Quelle jolie robe, Marie! Est-ce celle que vous avez (tu as) fait faire à (par) votre (ta) soeur?* »

22. « *Oui, c'est une robe que je peux porter n'importe où, à n'importe quelle heure du jour (de la journée). Voulez-vous (veux-tu) venir avec moi au concert ce soir?* »

23. « *Non, je ne peux pas. Je n'ai pas le temps d'assister à un concert cette semaine, parce que la semaine prochaine je dois aller (il faut que j'aille) à Paris pour étudier.* »

24. « *Oh, vous avez (tu as) oublié de me donner votre (ta) nouvelle adresse. Voulez-vous (veux-tu) me la donner maintenant?* »

25. *Michel étudiait depuis une année à l'Université de Caen en Normandie.*

26. *Il avait vu beaucoup de belles choses, de vieilles églises, des villes intéressantes, et des peintures magnifiques.*

27. *Il pensait que la Normandie était une des provinces les plus pittoresques qu'il avait jamais vues, avec ses maisons anciennes et ses ports charmants.*

28. *Tous les jours il allait à son petit café préféré près du vieux château pour retrouver (rencontrer) ses amis.*

29. *Joséphine, dont le grand-père était français, est allée à Paris en avion avec sa cousine Sylvie pour y passer le mois d'avril avec des ami(e)s.*

30. *Elles ont visité les musées les plus célèbres, les beaux jardins, et les monuments superbes tels que la Tour Eiffel.*

31. *Un jour on a donné à sa cousine des billets pour la Comédie Française, et elles et quelques-un(e)s de leurs ami(e)s ont vu une des pièces de Molière.*

32. *Elles regrettaient beaucoup le départ à la fin du mois, ayant apprécié les bon repas et les expériences merveilleuses qu'elles avaient eus.*

33. *Suzanne et son ami Paul étaient des étudiants américains à une grande université.*

34. *Ils apprenaient le français depuis quelques années pour pouvoir aller en France avec leurs camarades (amis).*

35. *Après leur visite Paul a dit: « Si seulement j'avais su combien il est plus agréable de pouvoir parler la langue d'un pays, j'aurais étudié encore plus. »*

36. « *Je ne suis pas sûre, a ajouté Suzanne, que tous les étudiants se soient rendu compte de l'importance qu'avait (qu'a eu) leur visite pour l'entente internationale.* »

37. « *Je serai toujours contente, a continué Suzanne, que nous ayons eu l'occasion d'aller voir la façon de vivre des autres (d'autrui) et de commencer à comprendre leur culture.* »

INDEX